DOUBLE OBLIVION OF THE OURANG-OUTANG

DOUBLE OBLIVION OF THE OURANG-OUTANG

HÉLÈNE CIXOUS

TRANSLATED BY SUZANNE DOW

WITH THE COLLABORATION OF LUCY GARNIER

polity

First published in French as *Double Oubli de l'Orang-Outang*
© Éditions Galilée 2010

This English edition © Polity Press, 2013

Polity Press
65 Bridge Street
Cambridge CB2 1UR, UK

Polity Press
350 Main Street
Malden, MA 02148, USA

ISBN-13: 978-0-7456-5390-7
ISBN-13: 978-0-7456-5391-4(pb)

A catalogue record for this book is available from the British Library.

Typeset in 10.75 on 14 pt Janson Text
by Servis Filmsetting Ltd, Stockport, Cheshire
Printed and bound in Great Britain by the MPG Books Group

For further information on Polity, visit our website: www.politybooks.com

CONTENTS

PREFACE

Fifteen years ago, in 2009, I found a cardboard Box lain dormant for over half a century in the depths of a cupboard in the house where I go to write, which turned out, just like its ancient double the Gold-Bug, to be the bearer of a treasure of whose existence I had known absolutely nothing. I could have died without ever having laid eyes on that Box again. Now, I can see myself again on that June day in 2009, aghast upon finding hundreds of pages, of varying thicknesses and dimensions, of the first of all my manuscripts which, however, I had thrown out, or so I thought, in 1964, or so I thought, at the time when in 1964 I was discovering with delicate jubilation the hundreds of faces of the manuscripts of James Joyce 'preserved' in the cardboard boxes of the Buffalo library. A still unravished treasure, I can see myself *today exactly* as in 1964, transported by an ecstasy of stricken wonderment, seeing it borne towards me by an overwhelming force. It is odd. In time, I will think of myself as having ceded to a supernatural authority, like the one that drove Mr Earnshaw, upon finding the unnameable Subject (subsequently named Heathcliff) on a Liverpool street, to take him home, *at once*. In all his life, nothing will have so exhausted him, he casts himself down into an armchair, begging all around him without exception not to approach him for he is, so to speak, dead, as well as mortal and murderous. All those around him are already lit up by the mortal emanations of the Subject. The Subject has a power all his own, stronger than those of all around him put together. What is striking is that the Subject, even as he is stationed in the middle of the study, is content to gaze around him, seeming astonished to be there, motionless, as if in truth he were not there, as if his sheath were set down in this place whilst his soul ran wild and uncoupled from reality in climes where oblivion, solitude and abandonment reign.

But I was telling you about a manuscript.

Now, this manuscript was that of a book, written in my hand perhaps, but otherwise not at all. I can see myself trembling with happy grief at the sight of innumerable traces drawn by the hand of my friend J. D. I had entirely forgotten. It was a little yellowed 'book', it looked to have come from the ends of the earth, and no one could have told me whence, towards whom, nor by whom it came. I began, I cannot recall how, to contemplate, or listen to, the disjointed murmurs of this manuscript. I believe that I believed I recognized certain voices. Besides, I was not alone in this voyage on the island of memory. I was in the company of a Society of those highly powerful People of Letters whom *nothing escapes*, those famous ghostly artists – Emily Brontë of course, Edgar Poe and so Charles Baudelaire too and therefore Charles Meryon, Kafka, I am forgetting some of course, but they will come back to me as long as we return to the path of the Box.

And what of the Ourang-Outang?

Within every sensitive soul (sailor, poet, invalid) there is always a great ape and a tomb. As long as none tries to relieve him of his razor blade, with which he signs, the Ourang-Outang is no killer. That man is gentle as a lamb as long as we believe in *his reality*. But if anyone should suspect that there is an Ourang-Outang in him, he cuts. There is also the fable of the *Monkey Who Becomes a Writer* in La Fontaine, but the Monkey there is only a baboon.

The brigands, the thieves who break into the house at night, the ghosts of whom you are afraid as you are getting into bed, are all descended from the Ourang-Outang. We are all of us afraid of ourselves.

You will have gathered by now that this story is an Ourang-Outang. We cannot blame him for the violence he does us. We have taught him how to use a razor blade, and he wields it to shave away at our hearts. The man who is a shadow of a man, the entirely innocent convict, he whom we cannot blame for tearing us limb from limb, for slitting our throats, for forcing us upside down up into the chimney, our extranatural hero, is this Story to which I drew closer, towards which I was drawn by my fate, I was eleven years old, when it was all over I went to see it at the zoological gardens, we all bore the scars, I clung onto the bars of the book, I stared at it in this barred proximity, I contemplated its eyes so very pale behind which the Unexplained lay sleeping for eternity. It was a neutral, de-commissioned pity for us all, the killed, the killers, the locked away, those driven mad by madness, those by unmadness, a soapwashed, disinfected pity enclosed us. The trickiest thing to decipher is the force of the force of attraction that has always commanded me not to shy away from the unfathomable, too-bright gaze of the Very Powerful. In the end, will I, consciously, have re-read the Story that nonetheless *was read*? For it was read by someone (in me) who had the strength that I have not.

When it is all over, we shut the innocent monster up in a big zoological box.

Hélène Cixous, 14 April 2024

PART I

'So I will have re-read it.' I instantly wrote that sentence. As one might write down a prophecy. Begrudging, yielding. That was the first thing I did in the moment that followed the Event. I doubted not that I could already foresee its most distant – or so I thought – and surprising consequences, and was already setting off towards the end. Naturally. Not only had it all already begun, with the vast and majestic sudden-ness of a dawning of the world, with a profusion of pasts still entirely present and richly adorned; more than this, it seemed to me, in that moment I was forewarned of the last of the *future events*. My state of mind: excitement and sorrow intermingled. The Box was still in the middle of the room, scalding. It could not escape me. I could not escape it. I thought to myself. It is I who have brought it into the centre of my life, I said to myself.

I was entirely given over to my sentence by now. I went towards it.

'So I will have re-read it.' No. The moment the sentence was written – 'will have', not 'would' or 'must' – I set fever-ishly about rewriting it. It's all in the intonation. Perhaps I ought to whisper it at the end of a breath, blast it out in a cre-scendo yell, pronounce it broken in the middle, shout out the last stolen syllable, or be wail it, in tone it, incredulously. And yet there is also a note of triumph, someone here has won out over someone or something, so I should give it emphasis, so I will have re-read it, exclaim it, *So I will have re-read it,* surprise it: 're-read it??', let it fall back down and gather in the descent a shower of sparks!!!!! or rather!!!!!!!! This has already been done. Here I remember the hand-written grief of Saint-Simon gravely mourning his wife so:

𝄞 𝆕 𝄢 𝆑 𝆕 𝆑 𝆓 𝆑 𝆕 𝄞 𝆑 𝆒 𝄞 𝆕 𝄞 𝆑 𝆓 𝆕 𝄞 𝆑 𝆕
𝄢 𝆑 𝆕 𝆑 𝄞 𝆑 𝄞 𝆒 𝄢 𝆑 𝆕 𝆑 𝆕 𝄞 𝆑 𝄞

I had seen this line of tears in the manuscripts room of the Bibliothèque Nationale de France, and I had wept. I was overcome with adoration for the memorialist whose finest sentence will have been the beyond of any sentence, a stream of *hand-drawn tears* lined up, all in a row, like severed heads on days of mourning. Like so: *𝄞 𝆕 𝄢 𝆑 𝆕 𝆑 𝄞 𝆑 𝆕 𝆓*

within the body of the writing, at heart height, a belt of tears in single file, in the last quarter of a long traditional page, remarkable for the regularity of the handwriting that gives the chronicle the look of a regiment, just as they sprang forth during the un-broken labour, they had awaited their turn to take up their place in line after two military lines and the words: '*un excellent off. gl. et un très galant hom*'[1] followed by a full-stop. They had at that moment, one after the other, been poured into the eternal treasure trove of literature. A tribute and unique example of the interweaving of life into writing – of life, which is to say of death, the arrival of the event and its instantaneous deposition. I counted them. There are thirty-four of them to the line. In addition to those, on the same line, in the margin, there are eight tears, the last of them hurried, withheld, shed. I should perhaps not count as a tear the sixteenth of them, which is drawn in the shape of a cross, but a cross with an open body that flows like a tear, it is a cross the same size as the neighbouring tears, of which there are fifteen on one side and eighteen on the other, each

---

[1] 'An excellent g.^{al} off. and a most gallant gentlem.'

trembled and fallen differently, thirty-three or -four tears, plus another eight in the margin, which makes forty-two tears including the cross, rendingly hewn, leaning to the left or right, contorting their own lines, choking themselves, breaking up, knotting; forty cries drawn up in a line, neatly collapsed, painstaking convulsions, a cemetery tragic in its veracity, its servility, admitted to the edifice of the narrative and not banished and penned in as is, save for exceptions, the fate of woes when they come to suspend the weave to which the author grants the privileges of fidelity. Of this splicing of the flesh there was nothing that could be related in letters, nothing that flows in words, but only in droplets and mucus. And yet those tears are letters wept, jewels of the alphabet of sobs, I said to myself, each one is the quintessence of a memory coming asunder, and I wept – with joy.

Next line: *L'Assemblée extraordinaire du Clergé qui finissait vint haranguer le Roi à Marly.*[2] He will not have wasted a single tear, I said to myself, nor a word.

I can see at this point that I shall need to add to the sentence 'So I will have re-read it' a note of mourning, the bejewelled hue of what one has lost. To hear in 'So I will have re-read it' the aura of regret at having thus ceased not re-reading. It's all there in the 'oh' of the *so*, sounding the death knell of grace. Soh/why. And with this I start following with variations the multiple music encapsulated in this endless sigh. 'In the end, I will have re-read' – I wrote – 'the book that I had thought never to re-open' and it seemed to me for a moment that this phrase, in its eschatological phosphorescence, had quite evidently to be stationed at the opening of the book that I had not yet begun writing, but whose slender young shadow had

---

[2] 'The extraordinary synod of the Clergy that was drawing to its end came to harangue the King at Marly.'

5

been following me for days now. Then it wavered and began again: 'The book that I had promised myself I would sooner die than read – in the end, I will have re-read it *so*.' Hurriedly, I set to once again, tried a form, flung out the re-adjusted sentence, (at)tempted another fate; fitful, laying siege to the fervour that straitened my heart from all sides, I tailed it with a spume of words, turning about the grievous spot, drunk with irrepressible imprecision, in hopes of finding a phrasing simple and powerful enough to bring together the conflicting anxieties to which the Event gave rise in me. (That is, the improbable Box's so unorthodox, seemingly cunning, entry into my life.)

(How far I have been caught off guard cannot be put into words. Without forewarning or foreboding, at least as far as I know, no omen, nor dream, at least as far as I recall: an Event has presented itself without intermediary, without messenger, in the most homely of fashions.

Naturally I cannot but perceive, a few paces behind today's astonishment, the Great Astonishment, that of the year 1996, to which this one might for a brief moment seem to be a reply. But while the principal magical accessory of the Great Astonishment of 1996 will have turned out to be a box, the events are in all aspects different, including the trigger. There are events, and boxes too. The box of 1996 was an old dirty blue box, the size of a shoe-box, but square, and which had never been in my possession nor, in truth, in the possession of my brother, its bearer, since he had, of his own accord, disappropriated himself thereof in another story. Whilst the Gold-Box neither reached me, nor was delivered, nor brought to me. It never ceased being there without being here. Until the moment when it *emanated*. And it is this moment that provokes me and calls me into question. Myself, the whole house, and so the theatre and temple of all my books, the setting for all my life's catastrophes and comedies. Had I forgotten it? No. Neither forgotten nor not forgotten. The Box is going to force me to rethink the subtle, so subtle concept of forgetting, I thought. I could already foresee a very feverish meditation on the Forgetting of Boxes (or the unforgetting – that is, the different forgettings and forgettances) awaiting me, flicking at a ream of paper with excitable fine, feline tails. I haven't thought about the box of 1996 since 1998, and it is the discovery of this so very different Box that brings it back from amongst the shadows.)

(Once again: I came back – let's say yesterday – to the house that is more than a house and less than a house since it is my writing chest –

it seems to be a house, with its little rooms, its narrow beds, its few cupboards, it has room enough for its occupants but is quite plainly booked out. Its permanent residents are my books, my true friends. My books, that is my friends, live in delightful society, which serves as a well-tended forest, a company of oracles, a protective cortège. By contrast the kitchen, through which I cannot help but pass, is the jumble of Capernaum itself – the locality where Jesus my mother exercises her healing powers beset as she is by the throng of objects sick with age and stiff with ailments and tics, whose unruly, unwashed, battered, profoundly righteous heap earns her – my mother – a reputation as an enchantress and glory as a worker of miracles.

But I'll get back to arriving at the house: when, yesterday, I reach it, as usual, after the annual shipwreck, I have nothing left, the head empty, the body broken, the heart heavy, I have lost battles, the world is strewn with excrement, I am in the ruined state of the survivor and near lifeless. But confident. 'I shall have a book' I tell myself. As unhappy as I may be and forever so the happy god is oakful with his train of squirrels. A pinecone is fired at my back. Fifty! Seventy! I count, on all my fingers, some come to me, others I borrow from friends. I have nothing and I shall have everything. Is this possible? Ah well, this nothing, this poverty, these ruins, these inures, I shall endure them willingly even as lifeless, so expected is it that I should expectantly await myself upon the coming of a book. I do not show my belly to those I meet; they would not believe me. Nor do I look at it myself. I scrutinize nature, mysterious mistress of resurrections. Whence shall it spring forth, the miraculous happening? Far away in the east winks the little red eye of the lighthouse, saying: believe! believe! believe! at regular intervals. I believe believe believe believe

(this does nothing to keep a terrible despair from crouching down in tears next to me) (the pain grows in screeching the deep blue expanse of belief)

It will come, I believe. I haven't even any curiosity. As if I were an incubating hen, distracted, patient, in the warm fullness of her divine henness.

And yet yesterday, the book that I was preparing to feel on its way from the outermost limits of the universe, at the moment when I saw myself seeing – as Stendhal perfectly did the white wall four kilometres from here at the moment that will have preceded – him crouched in white trousers on that mountain – ridiculously named *Janiculum* – the crystallization of the book that will come to me – far from being out on parade, roaming free in castles in forests beneath a few cloths of white cloud, it was already as close as could be. The

Book. I could almost have been sitting on it unbeknownst to
me.)

$$\mathcal{f}$$

I would so have liked.

I would so have liked a great many things. And in the end in
vain. I would so have liked to have drawn out of my trembling
the sentence with so fine a head, so long and supple a neck,
the very image of a rose the very image of an arrow which, in a
single stroke, would paint true the singular sharp of a sunder-
ing. I was indeed sundered. Stripped, split and slashed.

I had The Box in my sights – I can hear myself.

I had sundered for myself the impassibility whereof I had
until this day – which seemed in no way destined to become
memorable – been able to attest to the solidity, quiet, constancy, sleepiness, withstanding all mistrust. You sleep and
suddenly you sink. It is 28 June, a Sunday, and we have struck
a rock. Interior. The Box is not to blame; it was sought out,
set upon. An interior, utterly inexplicable event. Suddenly we
sink beneath time's cubits.

To myself I say: 'So I will have re-read it.' Myself judge,
accused and executor. This might be laughed, blushed, wept,
scoffed at. A sententious, bitter stench. To throw oneself on
a Box in the early hours and eviscerate oneself. The accident
gave off such a force of death – or else of life –, such a Force
– that I was thrown stuck onto this moment that had caught
me in its brutal amber as in myths where one sees people
captured in a salt or in the plaster of immortality. Women
mostly.

I would so have liked swiftly to have shared this scorching with my friend. I would have said to him: 'I have just found . . . !' without having to hide the untidy flow of my emotions. He would have said: . Then I would have said: . He would have said: we'll figure it out. Par excellence. And timidly and heartened, I would have started to confide in him what I would have had great difficulty admitting to myself:

And so he would have said: par excellence. And I would have believed him without hesitation.

But he had just left.

I would so have liked to tell my son the astrophysicist of this utterly meteoric accident, reckoning that he would provide me with the astral or subterranean metaphor, which would help me to bear the real, dense darkness that the object's quasi-fall had unleashed in my head. But he had left a few minutes before what I experienced as an explosion, a fracturing of the universe that he had just set up around me, by setting all the parameters of the onboard instruments, so that I could embark on my virtual voyage in the safest, most modern fashion. Never before had I been as methodically technologified. Everything had been more or less pre-planned by my son the pre-pilot. And so the box had emerged with the dazzling slow majesty of a sperm whale, *very like a whale* joked Hamlet, who roams around my mind as he does his castle, and it was not at all 'very like a whale'. *It was a* whale. A bull whale. I will not for an instant have doubted that the Box was male. It was entirely male. All its parts, all its sexes were male. I hadn't thought. It is now, as I begin to record the report of the Event, that this occurs to me, as the unmistakable is detected only after the fact. I must instinctively have felt the effect of this male-diction. I was disquieted, rather silenced: the sensation I had was of the absolute exteriority to the foreign continent that was the Box even though it presented itself as a part of myself and came from myself, which I did not deny. A son might seem just as clearly detached. Not mine. The fact that my son should have just left a minute before I needed to use him as a paternal analyst is just like me, just like him. It was just fine.

I would so have liked to tell my mother about the extraordinary and picturesque event for which one of her wardrobes had just acted as the theatre, I would have fixed her a story spiced to tempt and hearten her, she would have sipped it with pleasure, but the Deafness Dragon that guards her cave insists that his captive be addressed only in bellows. Yet my story can only be murmured the length of a silence. Therefore I must also forgo her commentary, which, always so fresh and unmatched, still reached me last summer like the most familiarly dazzling reading all the way from a free star. And lit up by her words I saw everything, differently. Instead of preparing her a sizzling secret report on the matter, I heat up her soup and swallow my passion.

She is eating more and more. I make a note of that on 1 June in my diary, by which I mean hers. I follow her progress day by day. When did it begin? The beginning escaped me. She told me in March: I'm eating more and more, she said. I didn't believe her. Eat, I said. I am constantly afraid of her melting away. Slight, slim, even skinny perhaps. Eat, I say. She obeys. She never fails to obey. Not out of servility but as an act of trust. It is me, which is to say her mother, whom she obeys. She never stops eating, says my brother. On the evening of 31 June I suddenly notice the size of her thighs. I had just taken off her yellow trousers and am holding her

11

pyjama bottoms out to her. That's when I can clearly see the new width of her thighs. It is not the effect of the sagging of the fabric. The light is flooding in through the window, yellow like the trousers, and lays an amber gold on her belly, her thighs, her knees, her legs. On the one hand, the day, which is setting in dusky golds – she goes to bed before seven o'clock in all her glory – gilds her and beneath a thick syrup my mother's flesh takes on the adorable depths of an old Rembrandt. On the other, the hour's lamplight illuminates the precise state of the body: the volume has unmistakably grown by about a third from the hips to the ankles. This discovery falls upon me like the gong of an apocalypse. Will she have gained weight from one moment to the next? Her swollen, shapeless face sunflowers towards me. The eyes shining, their sparkle more vivid and jolly for having to pierce matter, laugh roundly at the feat: she reads my expression. Ha! Ha! laugh the eyes.

At first the idea of her gaining weight frightens me. Then I am frightened by my fright.

I can hear within me the outrageous tone of outrage: Mum has just gained weight. It is something incongruous and quite unexpected. If ever there were a constant so perfectly uninterrupted in my life that I lent it as little doubt as the repetition of the rising of the sun, it was the fact of my mother's unchanging slenderness. The whole family's equilibrium rested upon this simple, vital, elegant fact. She has always been a scale, upright and true as a beam. My mother, I say to myself, cannot gain weight. And so another woman has taken her place. Not only has she gained weight, she is gaining weight. You'll have to get used to it, I say to myself. I speak to myself without conviction. More precisely: she is eating. Before – a before that seems lately to have mockingly set in – she simply took in sus-

12

tenance. She was always a model of agile sobriety, effortless, with the economy of a born dancer. On 3 July, as I present her with a lunch tray suited to her desires and needs, with nothing forgotten, the daily sausage chopped up into even slices in the soup, she says: something's *missing*. What? A small glass of red wine. 3 July will have been the first day of the lunchtime glass of red wine at the age of 99. She watches me pour. I leave the bottle on the table. 'One glass is enough,' says my 3 July mother. A loving sadness weeps within my heart: I'm mourning my mother from before 3 July. Something tells me that she won't ever be back. On the other hand, there is never a dull moment, I say to myself. With Eve, there are always surprises. On the one hand I want nothing ever to change, on the other I like a clean sweep. Eve was forever patching the world up and out, stringing it along with her magic wand. She is the artist of the stick and length of string who invented the first window-stops. Take a broom-handle once it has lost its mop of hair through over-use. Slice it up into equal rounds. Make a hole in each segment and thread a bit of string through – thirty centimetres will do. Every window in the house bears my mother's signature. A broom-handle's spin-offs are a political manifesto. Never let go.

I savour the tricks that she pulls out of her wand. In the middle of the previous sentence the sound of a fallen cane rang out. I answer the call. The cane is also the house phone, the bell, the sceptre, the conductor's baton, the statue of my mother in all her legendary slenderness, the rigid and malicious trait of her character, the flute that accompanies her rickettiness and charms the pack of the stairs to heel.

The glass of red wine calls for an interpretation. It is hidden behind the immediately available, superficial explanation – that my mother perhaps believes in the virtues of a drop of alcohol to fortify what remains of youth in old age, or else to re-kindle a slight poetic inebriety. But that's not it.

I do not yet know the mother who eats, drinks, gains weight and who is being born of my mother who is passing. She changes fast. My mother who this year will have become my grandmother and soon my great-grandmother and thus my tiny child has boarded without me this ghost train of old age which, after a certain station, suddenly brutally speeds up. And yet just lately she is eternal. She exceeds my imagination.

'Fourcolours!' cries my mother.

She gobbles up the geraniums with a kind of enthusiasm in her eyes: she never tires of the fact that the flowers raise their stems in four quite different colours. Each day soup, sausages, geraniums . . . the combinations of different lives. I see her enthralled by an ecstasy come from as far off as time regained, and I recognize her, the wondrous woman who reigned during the season of early childhood and whom we have woefully lost. She regained, what? The colour red of the geraniums which is not the same red as the red of the other plant, the colour red of the colour red of red

I realize that I resent this ashen Box like a being that hails from a world without colours that mocks my anxieties of a girl threatened by the immense forgetting that will come to devour the brightly coloured kingdom

I say: Box. I dream for an hour or two about the Box character. Cardboard is always for me the metonym of the cardboard box. I say: 'the box, he . . .' rather than 'she' or 'it'. I do not consciously choose the thing's gender. The gender imposes itself upon me. What if I were to tinker with the object with a few psychoanalytic tools – saying of an empty box once filled that she is a masculine box – but I don't want to go on with this. The word-thing Box dives into all the Boxy places and scenes. I could write the history of one of our lives of the last century from the point of view of the Boxes' journey. My family's whole history is a series of uprootings preceded or pursued by boxes. At each stopover, from Ithaca to Germany as far as the Last Extremity we have to leave boxes behind. It is the lot and the structure. Take the *Endurance*: Shackleton – and his twenty-eight sailors – sails from Ithaca, New Zealand, with hundreds of boxes. He cannot do otherwise. Crossing the Antarctic continent in two years or ten years means setting out with ten or two years' worth of boxes of provisions. The hundreds of boxes are the advance proof that the Antarctic of time has already been mentally crossed. He has known since Ulysses that he will shed a load of boxes from islet to islet at each icy stage. From the moment of 'boxing up', what has been entrusted for safekeeping is already given up. What is beautiful is that we *sincerely* think we are saving what we have just condemned. The word *sincerely* has always been the most unbelievably unqualifiable of modalizers. We say it to swear good faith, and the very fact of swearing good faith, and of qualifying faith that is neither good nor bad, has already poisoned the protestation. As soon as someone is sincere he is the surest of self-deceivers.

That day I decide to equip my mother with *South: The Endurance Expedition* for the crossing of the summer towards the hundred Pole. On the cover of the fat blue book by Sir Ernest Shackleton is an exacting photograph, almost unbearable in its inhuman exoticism. In the background and to the left of the image, gilded and shrunk by the perspective, like the dream of a scaled-down model, the delicate silhouette of the ship which during its lifetime was the *Endurance* is the size of a five-centimetre insect. All around it millions of forty to one-hundred metre icebergs ripple *into infinity*. One insect against a million monsters. An unbearable landscape that Ulysses could never have seen without fainting in horror. Not one person in the world could believe that one could 'cross' the Antarctic. But I am not looking at the photograph. My mother is four years old at the start of the famous, totally humanly impossible attempt. Another three years of surhumanity, I say to myself. I am not thinking anything in giving her this book like a biscuit tin for the crossing except that this hardback volume is thick enough and contains hundreds of incidents that will serve as newspaper and television since she has entered a cold and distant domain where newspapers and television cannot reach her attention. A few weeks later, as if I had made it far enough away from a dream for it to become suddenly legible, I understand that the entirety of this work is an allegory of mum. I do not follow her into the Antarctic since you have to be one of a hardy breed to set out into such long wintry temperatures. It suddenly occurs to me that the photograph represents my mother's interior landscape. The *Endurance* with its stiffened arms, its motion held fast by the ice for months, and most of all, all the world's colour violently turned white and anticolour in its tiny frame – that's her.

But the Box himself as a body does not deceive. There will never be astonishment enough at his endurance – these animals have extraordinary resistance. They do not decompose. They are not eaten by worms and moss. They only die if they are killed. They can bear a hundred times a thousand times their weight.

On the comic side, the thought of the Box, the moment I tack it seriously, is accompanied by a tune that my mother liked to whistle, whose tangy charm she had discovered as a young German girl learning French. She would sing 'Mrs Box

16

is missing her boxes, her box is missing her . . .' I was three and I found it delightful that the syllables could be sent flying like that, without knowing it I found my way into homophony thanks to Boxes-missing; and not only that. I had a foretaste of the metamorphosis of things in name and vice versa.

When one day soon I will ask my mother – whom I find sitting wrapped up in shawls and dressing gowns on the balcony with the scalding geraniums – where, in which boarding house for young German girls in Paris, she had heard and learnt that musical jig, she doesn't understand what I am talking about; in vain I pluck out the syllables one by one but Mrs Box has sunk into eternal oblivion. My mother smiles kindly, no, she doesn't know the street, she is not from around here.

Everyone has gone, and the Box is back. I say to myself. Later I shall wonder if there was a causal link between these two movements.

At the moment I am missing everyone and everything, and everyone and everything has become this old Box that is still quite big and sturdy, blackened with a dust that acts as a dirty beard, seemingly still, solid, listless and yet stormy, I thought, I put my mother methodically, lovingly, swiftly to bed, and I thought of the Box. This is the time when we talk to one another the least, we act, in concert, she raises her arms, I pull on the pullover of skin, for she has already taken out her ears and can no longer hear anything but the language of eyes. 'Shall I take off the blanket?' I ask with my eyes and she cries yes yes; without the ears the voice drops, cries, squawks, tumbles. 'The newspaper!' she cricries. I take *Le Monde* and lay it on the floor under the bedpan. The yellow day coats it with a golden finger. It is lovely.

'So *silly*, being old!' She burstscries out laughing. 'No escaping it,' she replies to herself. She says: so *silly being* old until the kneaded, softened phrase is no more than a ribbon of elastic gold silibeingold. We laugh. Savour the joke. Beingold. 'I wasn't like this,' she notes. 'When?' 'Last year.' She keeps a diary too, I note – a virtual one. 'I think,' she ponders, 'that I wasn't like this last year.' 'That's true,' I say. That reassures her. She is not mistaken. Mustn't complain. She keeps herself company. But, she says, it's so *Silly* being old. It just happened. I am old says my mother. She lets me know. 'Your daughter is in America?' 'Yes.' We make a whistle-stop world tour in thoughts, non-stop. Mum's self shattered into fragments on all the continents, we put it all back together, not forgetting anyone, 'and the cats? they aren't wetting the bed?' 'No,' I say. 'Now-I-hope-you-sleep-well.' This sentence is the ninth in the liturgy and the last. To close, the voice laughs: so Sssillly! We laugh. The word Sssilly is clothed in a gilded, joyful tone. The Box is crouching above my head. It weighs me down. Through the floorboards, the ceiling, down at the bottom, as if it were waiting for me in its bedchamber. So Ssilly Beingold. It is without colour without number without make-believe. My mother raises her standard and cries: 'Fourcolours!'

'Every book is an illness from which I'm trying to recover,' my friend had said to me. When the book is half-done, I feel half-dead. He had smiled. At half-book you are half-way along the path that leads from life in death to life in life or the other way around.

Whereas for me every book is a kind of child that cures me from nothingness, said I. I could say that of all the books I had read, except the one whose Remains now lay in the Box.

Of that one I could have said that it had been like an illness but I never spoke about it.

Was it a book? Nothing but a book, purely a book, only a book? I doubted it even before it came out. I can't remember a thing about its gestation. A mass of foreign memories surrounds it. Some of them may be real memories. They all seem to me to be posthumous fabrications. It was an object of fear.

You'll find a portrait that looks like it. On my bookshelves.

I saw it, when it so happened in days gone by that I would catch a glimpse of it, inadvertently, for I always avoided meeting his face, as a dirty child with black hair that formed a dark veil over the forehead, in rags and flea-ridden, across the shoulders too like an ermine of flimsy rags, the face illegible as ancient, seemingly homeless and yet as homely as could be, veiled right down to its speech, for it tirelessly repeated its earnest gibberish – and each time I had this intense feeling of déjà vu that distastefully unsettles inner ease: now here is someone, I sense, or something foreign, whose foreignness is not foreign to me, that I must have forgotten, that requires me, a barbarian who seems destined for-addressed to me –, who returns to me, and the entirety of whose aspect arouses a fearpity, a feeling improper for avowal, a criminal revulsion, the wan bitterness of an ingratitude. He is instantly recognizable: *the child of reproach*. It is always a case almost of a 'foundling', which is to say a lostling, thus of what is called, to keep the truth at bay, a 'foundling' when in fact we will never stop losing it. Most of all it is a broken off piece of Obscurities, a stone across the way, a pebble in the shoe, an interloper of whom none can unburden us. A remember-you-will-kill. And since we do not know his real name we give him as a pseudonym the name Pseudonym. To call to him we use the name of a son who died young, and we do it in the grip of one of the Obscurities, with the redoubtable lightness of a blind man who does not know that he cannot see himself killing himself. Once we shall call him Heathcliff, and this is not a name but a precipice ushered into the dining room. Heathcliff is the collective pseudonym in gibberish for all the foundlings who have spectralized my bookshelves ever since I could read. And even as they are the masters of different dramas, it is always the same black son who returns. This much I know. However, the different fathers who find the veiled child in different cities know nothing of one another.

He who picks up a pebble in a Liverpool street does not know that the same father takes in the same son fallen from the lap of fate on the Ragusa road. The child veiled by misfortune answers no questions, naturally. The father's maternal heart is a nut that the child cracks between his teeth. This Heathcliff's false name is Nicolo, otherwise known as Colino, the sobriquet of the plague. In every case the Precipice exerts a supernatural authority over the father. He becomes, within three weeks, three days even, the father's Scar. There must be an explanation. I cannot deny that I experience the Box's return in accordance with the hypothesis of a Foundling case. The cardboard veil holds fast.

8

'What is sad' I thought – as if the sadness could not be mine, but as if there floated over the subject of this book a sad mist that touched me – is that if it is a book, it will have been the first and it won't have been happy. Tis pity. But even this melancholic affect is perhaps no more than a borrowed memory. That I should have been driven to borrow melancholy, and from whom – there lies the problem. Quite the contrary, I do not doubt one bit that it was loved, more even than loved, decidedly loved and not by me, and even decisively loved, by an inaugural act and later more than an act, by my friend the poet. Precisely this 'book', with regard to which I shall always be in disarray, is the one that my friend – independently of any influence, and taking no account in advance and on principle of the numerous statements that escort a book towards catastrophe, and all the more so when it is a matter of a book that emerges from the wilderness by crawling for the first time – will have chosen without delay, immediately, and once and for all.

This was my reasoning: since he could love that which I could not 'love', and since I did not doubt him, whereas with regard to myself I was only ever in absolutely inexorable doubt, I would trust him rather than myself, without altering my feeling, but out of need for respite. This took place at a time when I *could* do nothing, except allow myself to be swept along by a frenzied impotence. I remember having been a nightmare, but that's from a fossilized memory. There was a little table where I, H., was seated, there was H., the 'thing', the 'fact', the 'vassal' before him, who was facing us. At least I can 'see' myself, but I can no longer see anything of him except the voice. In 1965. The date I don't remember – I'm piecing it together from the archives. I am the woman in a photo taken in the city by a professional photographer. It was there that my friend began explaining to me how there is a *tight* link between Ovid's *Metamorphoses*, those of Dionysius the Areopagite (who was always someone else and even someone from another era, since he is on the hill of the Areopagus when Saint Paul gives his sermon, whilst being in Syria in 490, and his writings illuminate the Middle Ages from the Abbey at Saint-Denis – a simultaneity of times explicable when in the shadows of mysticism), and the metamorphoses of my inner characters, about which I preferred not to *know* anything. He emphasized the word *tight*, and the fact that all truth lies in the *tightness* of one's own name, in the fact that it is always a pseudonym. And more than once over, too. I can still see it, along with the book's yellow or boxwood-root cover. For love of fine literature (as opposed to the pseudo-fine) he championed metamorphoses more readily and in preference to the sombre horrors of the Pseudo Old Testament and we read the loves of Pyramus and Thisbe in the version performed in *A Midsummer Night's Dream*, where it is shown that it is possible to see voices and take pleasure in the most excruciating suffering. It may be that one of the

22

foregoing sentences is not by me but by one of my doubles. Doubt is allowed. In any case, for the first time in my life I sensed that it could be not unpleasant to be all at sea or even, as sometimes happens to me, to have one's bag stolen with all the papers inside, ID, money, keys – the things that make up a person –, as a result of having left it unattended on a chair for stealing, by a thief you catch in the act without managing to retrieve your own bag from her.

The metamorphosis that Stendhal, for his part, liked best was the one about Daphne being turned into a laurel-bush. Whether he sees himself as Daphne, the laurel-bush, or Metamorphosis he does not say. He does not name the other roles. He says he likes, or only likes, 'she who flees even the name of lover'. Many (men) desire her; she slips through their fingers, she roams woods impenetrable to men, for whom she cares not; chastity, love, marriage . . . she pays no heed. Her father is forever telling her: 'You owe me a son-in-law, my girl! A son-in-law! Grandchildren!' he says, over and over. 'You owe me children, my girl!' She: (as if to a crime, refusing the bonds of marriage) Ah! If only he could be her! 'In reality', for his torment he is the hunter fled. Henri. In truth, he revels in the fugitive's extreme speed. Daphne, the timely virgin, is his secret role. It is in the fleetingnesses of love that he dreams his dreams. *Altera* is his secret first name. It was perhaps in 1794 when Henri not yet but already Stendhal found out the truth of Ovid's *Metamorphoses*. He is 11 years old, the first year of love of the first love. All this is hidden away in the text. He is not Apollo, he is Daphne, her own wife.

When my friend explains the non-conjugal relations between the different metamorphoses, I see the link. In 1965 I wanted at all costs to be someone else. I can see myself devouring *Metamorphoseon* in Latin, because I didn't read, I suckled, I ingested, I was earlier fed on Freud and Shakespeare, Ovid's sucklings, and I had already read, with great passion, his issue, Montaigne, before having read him, exile's changeling, returned from Augustine's disgraces to be turned into the King's protégé. I owe it all to Ovid – children, books, crimes, evasions and consolations. Ovid, Consolation's first name. When I am cast down into Hell, or the poisonous humiliating hole from which there is no escape of the *taedas conjugales* and where you know that hope – the last breath of mortals – cannot enter and where you shiver from cold, all I have to do is read one page, any page, of one of the books of *Metamorphoses*, and in the passage from one line to the next I am drawn out of Hell and brought back to the other world where there sings the genius whose name is Freedom.

In those days I was a larva, I was hibernating in damp caves, I would wake up in soiled sheets, I was living in excessively ancient houses whose incomprehensible subdivisions were such that, rather than losing one's way trying to move from floor to floor via corridors that lead now down, now up by turning, turning back on themselves, one had only a single thought, which was that one of these passages finally takes us back to the hideaway that we had had the ill-fated desire to leave behind us, as if in a mind aflame. Once I had taken flight, I had found myself, the moment I escaped from this building, before the face of a mountain that I had to climb as quickly as possible, before the sounding of the alarm, I was wearing pretty black patent high-heeled shoes, my only item of distinction, and I threw them away so as to grip the ground with my bare toes. Having reached the pass, I did not have the strength to lift my legs to make the metre between me and the other side. I had to reconcile myself to waking up in the gloomy chamber. I would so have liked to have been changed, but then, at that time, I so dreaded being turned into an ant-hill that I would not have breathed a word about it. I may have recovered from the horror I suffered from in this Middle Age of my life, but I have retained a revulsion for words in *gr*. I am always afraid that such a word might start scuttling about in the darkness.

The Box might date from that ice age. In those dark days I can say that I was sometimes given to acts of writing, in great secrecy, and initially in secrecy from myself. These deeds – they cannot be spoken of as work – were a kind of piracy. Deeds, bad ones it seemed to me – reprehensible, incomprehensible. Not to be spoken of. Let's not speak of them. Nothing would have been more disturbing to me than to have heard them speak. They occurred at night, in silence and in secret, and they were nothing to do with me. What have they done now? I would say to myself, when, getting down to work in the mornings, in my academic's office, I would discover traces of outlaws in amongst the meticulous and tightly bound pages of my thesis work. I seem to remember that I was in fact an eager, conscientious teacher, extremely demanding of myself. All memory, order, light, speed, sense of direction, domestic and professional administration were on my side. On the side of the teacher. As a larva I was on the side of waste in all its forms: detritus, slough, dross, vomit, dejecta, fumes, scraps of paper, I lay seedlike in the rubble, I went in filthy dreams beyond the admissible, I splashed about between urine and faeces and I would not be born.

And yet the Box is remarkably well turned out. Another of fate's little jokes, I say to myself, these reliefs of misfortune tidied away in a golden chest?

Why was I setting about the ruins on this particular June day so eagerly awaited for months, day of dreams, day of rediscovery of my sanctuary where I hoped to wrest myself from the debris and chaos of the real city so as to set up camp 'in the literary heights', as I promised myself, painting myself a brightly coloured fiction-heaven in which I believed. Why, when I was dreaming of raising myself up above the oaks and pines after a swift metamorphosis whose prototype could be found in the pages of my Ovid, had I lowered myself, in the hour that followed my rejoining the family in the writing chest, and even wallowed in the remains. I had immediately swerved from my aim, vital as it was, I had bowed to an obscure and inaudible law, an hour after I had arrived I had crept on all fours beneath the rickety table, I had swaddled its feet in felt shufflers, and come upon such a mass of spiders' webs and dust burs that I had to start sweeping up, and so also to sweep the broom closet, and to set about the heap of vile and decaying objects that glutted the whole cavity, and I had given myself over to the demon of interment.

So it was that I came upon the Box.

ᔕ

'Fourcolours!' My mother's cry cuts across the day. Judders. Is brought up short before the Box.

I translate: Four cull-hours.

She is right. The Box is the first of four blows struck this Hour 2009. The mood suddenly takes me to go to Montaigne's Tower, it is the time of the year known as Montaigne-Tower-o'clock when I go there to inscribe my name in the Register of Literature. The mood lifts me up. Puts me back down. I shan't go, I thought. The time has come, I said to myself, to revisit the Tower in memory. The idea that I shan't go to the Tower draws back, pales, silently shrinks away. I stay back alone with the Box. The Box gets bigger.

When? The very same day after the evening I came back, which was the forty-fifth return to the library that acts as my writing house. The forty-fifth of the new year's days.

A box hermetically sealed by brown paper sticky-tape, unbroken. Inviolate.

Where? At the bottom, to the left, right on the floor, in the darkness of the narrow linen cupboard sunk into the darkness of a gap in the partition walls between two bedrooms kept for the children. It is dingy in this cubbyhole. The sheets are piled up like archival collections, in disorder of the periods to which they belong. Old sheets, some very, some large, white coarse linen sheets never used and originating from an idea of virginity that my Spanish grandmother had of her dowry, always kept without thinking. Underneath. Below the shelf. A little further towards the back. *There*: lurking. Dormancy of a volcano. A spot that will have secured the secret. This cupboard is the only one to escape all lighting. This cupboard has the swarthy features of a cardboard box. Tight-lipped. Withdrawn. Uninviting. The two locks stare, non-committal, into the void.

Since when? According to my research, since 1966.

Introduction to the Box: Good condition. Dimensions: 50 × 29 × 32. Large red capitals in English: *VALUABLE BOOKS: Keep dry*. A real cardboard box, well presented. Professional. *Valuable books*. Distinctions are made between valuable books and other books. Valuable books. Precious books of no commercial value, priceless. Cherished. Books held in esteem. Books feared. Books of flesh. Books that you gave me.

Creatures of the heart. What are the values of great value? Of very great value? In any case, the Box is undeniably of value. Keep the box? Occasionally we will have kept old purulent, modest, economy boxes – whatever the value of the value of the contents. The Box was a superior box. Reserved for superior books. And now?

These days the Box bears, on the right-hand flap in very large handwritten letters, in red ink, in a column from top to bottom: *Jeffers/ Prénom/ de Dieu/ Ms/ Gr*. In my hand. Steady, animated script. Tall, authoritarian letters. Like a decree. Everything in the body of the letters seems to say: touch me and I'll shoot.

Apparent coherence: what is announced belongs to the same period of my existence. 1964. The year when everything will have begun, unbeknownst to me, either to be finished or begun. 'Jeffers le Prénom de Dieu': read by an innocent archivist, nebulously promising. Read by me, it makes up a fabulous hypothesis beyond all objective knowledge. Who knows?? I had never thought of it, but the suggestion is not without value. As the statement passes before my eyes, in its accidentally cabalistic form, a fable crystallizes within me. A note of wonder lands on the old name of Jeffers, which has been uttered around me a mere two or three times in the last forty years, that is, since 1968. I see it in this moment as the mummy of a sovereign known only to a small number of archaeologists. It is a code name. A password between myself and the Californias, all Californias. Excavated: 1964. Then Postexcavated: 2009. What was ever the link between 'Jeffers', God, and one of God's first names, if such there were before the Box?

Who? Jeffers. 'God's First Name.'

Jeffers? I owe to Jeffers. Unable as I am to evaluate what I owe to Jeffers, I suspect that I perhaps owe him much more than I think and seem to owe him. What arouses my suspicion is the silence and banishment in which I – handed over? abandoned? – handed over into the care of an infinite negligence the character of Jeffers. Jeffers has always been a fiction. I have always used Jeffers, he has only ever been for me pretext and Subterfuge. When I decided to use Jeffers I had not a moment's hesitation, did not yield in the slightest to what might have subsequently developed into remorse or gratitude. I only ever had good feelings towards him, lukewarm, moderate feelings. This is no doubt to do with my initial decision to make of Jeffers a means to achieve my desire's true goal. The one I wanted to get close to and with whom I had categorically resolved to link my existence was of course James Joyce. I ought to reproach myself for only having turned to Jeffers so as to go through him in order to get back to Joyce as quickly and as surely as possible, but in 1964 the idea did not occur to me for a moment and now time has turned into fiction what once bore the furtive features of an unconscious design.

With Jeffers I pretended, but I should like to point out in his favour that I did so with care, courtesy and the utmost honesty. I took as my model Elvira, the young bride of the wealthy worthy goods merchant from Rome, Antonio Piachi, who loves as well as one can love without love her elderly husband. I always liked Jeffers, and all the more so perhaps because I was not bound to him by the 'bonds of marriage'. Besides, he was a handsome man, sombre and colossal. I could if I have time write a book or a chapter about this double-in-spite-of-himself. The incongruous feature of this matter is that Jeffers was one of a kind, the bard of the Very First, and ultimately an absolutely unique poet, even as, institutionally, he was always for me the Secondary; Joyce the Principal, Jeffers the Secondary. Nonetheless, I can maintain today that he will have remained absolutely unique as Secondary to Joyce, for not a single soul could have imagined that there might be a link between the two poets. That pair have only ever met in my head. And later in the Box. When I arrived on the doorstep of Hawk Tower he had just then made his entry into the book of the dead, in his own inimitable fashion, which is to say transformed into a falcon as planned.

It occurs to me that Jeffers would probably have appreciated the Box as a connoisseur, had he known. The man was the precursor of poetic ecology, but naturally we knew nothing about it, neither him nor I, in that corner of the world of the untamed 1960s. A box light, sturdy, solid as a rock, marginal, somewhat superhuman like a portable coffin.

Does the Box contain the 'thing' that it proclaims, inscribed in large, bold letters by my hand? (I must have been driven by an Energy when I traced those letters, either concealment or desire for vengeance, for the affect is legibly triumphant.) I doubt it absolutely. This sturdy doubt will have lasted not only until the opening of the box, but even an hour afterwards, up until the complete extraction of the documents.

ʃ

I ENTER THE BOX

I cannot remember what state I am in when I begin my visit. Let's say that a trance very quickly takes hold of me, a sort of hypnosis, for *I can see myself* unpacking very quickly and very mechanically, as if in a dream, as I would climb down or back up the steps of time, a steady flight, sleepy but systematic, ploughing ever onwards, ever deeper, an explora-tory expedition from one floor of the subterranean sky to another until I ended up bringing to light at the bottom of the box another powder-blue box whose contents I am unable to convey here. I shall call the undisclosed article '*Cour* Blue Box' (after the name of the luxury boutique that wrapped customers' purchases in lavish packaging, of which I have the most precise recollection, and which vanished without trace from the city some decades ago. Vestiges of this boutique inhabit wardrobes to this day), and this as long as I have taken no decision as to the fate of the Thing. Is it to be destroyed? Yes – unless there be an alteration (impossible now but unpredictable in the future), painful at first then less so, of my strong feelings concerning it. Nothing short of a tribunal will have to be staged to arrive at a verdict. Besides, the Thing, for the most part, together with a large quantity of documents relating to it, some quite recent and seemingly emitting murderous rays, are now kept in various containers that I am able very precisely to locate, without ever approaching them, much less touching them, indefinitely held in the nether-world of my memory. I note that I distinguish the liquidation of the remains from the Worst. I hereby close the provisional coffin of the buried alive.

I would have liked for this Cour blue Box not to be joined together and almost hidden, insinuated into the treasure's ulterior motive. I am nonetheless the author of this parcel. If I could pay myself a visit in another time, like Stendhal calling in on Montesquieu in another world to ask him: 'So? What should I make of myself?,' I should not miss the occasion to ask her, she who I no longer am, with what intention or by virtue of what state of mind could I have placed together treasure and dregs? Have I not always known the vast and troubling powers of contamination? Could I have exposed the treasure to tarnish? This could only be had I, at the time, considered the treasure already contaminated. So it was not a treasure. We alter. Long after, after great sadness, followed by revolts and coolings-off, we delight in what once aroused suspicion in us. I have died a triple death. I am today the legatee of the bags and corpses that I have bequeathed myself.

Initial inventory

I bring up bundles of typed and carbon copies of texts that I am aware of having written but which I have never read, typed single-spaced in several identical copies that I can, without difficulty, not-read. Reading-without-reading, an art-form that I have developed at the same time as my art

32

of reading – a technique perhaps, one skill within all those exercises that come under the heading 'reading'. That is how I can read a page in a single glance, as long as it is poetic, sensual, overwoven. The page in its entirety comes to be scanned in the cardiac organ of my brain in a tenth of a second. I can then play the page back from memory as the violinist does the score. I can equally not-read at any given moment such-and-such a piece of text that I will have experienced as undesirable, and at the same speed. When dealing with obnoxious plays, poisonous articles, pages obscene in their pretension, hypocrisy, vulgar rags, I distance myself at the same time as making their acquaintance, the deciphering and effacement are almost simultaneous. Naturally I share this capacity with a few others. In a flash one can see, read everything, and have neither seen nor read anything, as Proust often complainingly noticed.

I saw without reading those slim volumes which I can make out by their immediately registered titles. They all seem to me simple, and opaque, mute, so to speak. *The Sphinx*, *The Lyre* – no doubt about it, they are names. Names of constellations. Of metro stations. All brief fleeting inconspicuous. They cannot be called titles. It was reassuring: they gave nothing away. The paper: peel. Some, the copies, the same, in a large brown envelope – an envelope on which I have written 'for Mme Sanvin'. The power of names: with these syllables she rises up, appears. A living image. I hadn't seen her since 1967. She is back as good as new, complete, her voice still a little rasping, the colour of her hair too, a woman who worked as much as she could over and above her university post. Her re-appearance, accompanied by a double: I later had a close friendship with a lady from the university's administration whom to this day I had not recognized as the exact double of Mme Sanvin. She did not shun me. The first. I trusted her with my insects, my worms, my larvae. Today I see only the calm and intrepid spirit of Mme Sanvin. She would go down into the mine where I painted my asphyxias without turning a hair. She, gathering up the wounded, bandaging without fail that charred flesh that I entrusted to her care, whom I had totally forgotten in the oblivion where I incarcerated myself. I am glad to be re-united with the ghost of Mme Sarvin, author of the primitive copies. She is forever seated, her legs crossed, her face marked by her life's hardships, next to my sarcophagus. I wonder whether she too has had a brain tumour, as did her double.

I note: a few (author's) corrections amongst the pages, and additions, quite a few, handwritten, seen not read, of half a page, sometimes more, often final. I was pleased at this: the naïve pleasure of a child jubilant at having found glass jewels buried in sand that she will give to her allegorical mother in capital letters, the Great Library.

(With this I note, secondly: *I can see myself again* today, this June day 2009, busy discovering a large collection – hundreds, maybe – of sheets of paper, of varying con- sistencies and thicknesses, whose disorder is the cause of a rapid succession of moods: a gale of excitement, surprise, of indifference followed by jubilation and vice versa, I can *see* myself *again* today *exactly* as I am in 1964, feverishly busy, slow-hurried-restrained, opening up boxes of pages of all sizes, 'belonging' to the James Joyce manuscript collection 'preserved' in the Buffalo University Library, a still unrav- ished treasure, and there I am, I can see myself, quickly and gently unveiling, greeting, celebrating, there I am tenderly ravishing, rifling through with delicate jubilation the hun- dreds of faces of these pieces of manuscripts, raised up into the virtual heights of Literature by the strange joys of initia- tion. The journey is always as surprising: you have to go down into the well, lower yourself down via the galleries, crawling and wriggling, and once you arrive at the very depths, the final underground chamber suddenly gives out onto the sky.

In 1964 I didn't even know that I was boring down in 1964, I was in a previousness whose future I did not know, I was floating, foetal, in the waters of Literature, an all-powerful and contented state that one enjoys before all enjoyment and which precedes the formation of memory. And yet it is not impossible that the memory of these fore-traces would be revived were the individual of the literary species to be granted the, accidental, opportunity to live once again and in another world the exact same scene.

At this very moment here is also in Buffalo. I see myself again.

I will be able to believe that I am now re-appearing, I was myself in the Box and I have leapt from it upon the breaking of the seals as in the magical process recounted in the *Arabian Nights*. That is very like me. No reason why I should not today be twenty-seven, I am not going to break the charm by hastily over-investing in the reality principle. This cannot last. I am wary of the paroxysms of passion that shook me in Buffalo.

In 1964 I am going to write but do not know it yet. When in Buffalo I live entirely in the mode of *going to*, without presentiment. The Box contains the vestiges of this tense that is so particular to the French language.

In Buffalo I gorge myself on Joyce's handwritten pages. If it has been written that I am going to write on the threshold of the Buffalo library the message has not reached me.)

Subsequent discovery of several stories, entirely handwritten on both sides of the paper.

I am overwhelmed with joy. This joy is pure innocence, without thought, pre-thought, after-thought, source and torrent. I make the most of it. I have just received the Gift, and no giver. Except the Box. The joy is so strong, a pure flow, nameless, wordless. A rare and pure example of happiness. About which I will be able to write once twenty pages of analysis are done with. Instead of these words 'joy' and 'happiness', which are the modest remains of jubilation followed by regret at the inability to speak when carried to the exquisite heights of elevation. A thunderclap. And already the perfect tense: I have been enchanted

I have been searching for the portrait of this Joy that takes its own breath away in the book of joys stronger than the joyousness that serves as my treatise on superlative states – that *Life of Henry Brulard* that serves as Stendhal's Survival. In moments of extreme passion, one can only take pleasure as another. I had a 'heavenly memory', as Henry Brulard would say, unburdened of the weight of Stendhal weighed down by Beyle, in this moment so necessary to Literature where he (him or the other) withdraws as an author in the face of a 'subject that surpasses the teller'. I see that I do not remember the surpassing *subject*, whereas I do remember the state of being surpassed. I also recall precisely that the admission of the surpassed teller recognizing himself as smaller than the surpassing is situated, by happy accident or out of the utmost refinement, more or less at the book's end. (I believe I remember that *the teller* is in italics on the page where it appears, like a foreign word it seems to me, which it is in fact. *The teller* is a character in an imaginary Molière play made up by Stendhal. That was always his dream – to be Molière. He sometimes spells it Motlière in the margin.[3] This 'teller' is a kind of Sosie.[4] A Stendhal so-called, so-told Brulard so as to surpass himself in secret.)

Such that the *teller*, no longer able to say anything, falls silent, but leaves that which is stronger than him entirely free to continue to surpass, which is the very image of Literature as Infinite. And yet to my surprise, when I take hold of the book, it opens, or I do, at page 144, on a paragraph that describes the pain that the subject experiences on seeing himself describing, poorly and with difficulty, the subject that he nonetheless experiences as heaven itself. Stendhal is writing about the 'heavenly stay in Les Échelles'.[5] The year is 1790 or 1791, we are seven or eight years old, the gods and their ladders have just been created for us. On that day happiness is sudden, complete, perfect but heavenly. One can only imagine, dream, beseech it, and feel it thinly smile. Happiness is but a check-word, a king-word, a cardboard king attended by a knavery of pawn-words, a voiceless phoney cockerel. And all Literature assembles to give the divine surpasser a leg-up the ladder. In the end, the superlative ambassador gives up, on page 144, all efforts to render in sentences the vision of heaven and suggests a compromise: in order to veil the white sun of his travels in Échelles, he will unfurl a few happy-memories to provide as little inaccurate an insight as possible into the heavenly objects. Obviously I recognize all of a sudden the strategy of negative theology. I had paid no attention to it during my earlier travels

---

[3] In French, "mot" means "word".
[4] Sosie is a character in the Molière play *Amphitryon*, who is a doppelganger of the God Mercury. The word also means look-alike in French.
[5] Les Échelles is a town in south-east France, not far from Grenoble. The word also means 'ladders' in French.

in Brulardia. But what mystifies me is the page, and the fact that it lies in the vestibule of heaven when I thought it at the exit, rather towards Saint-Bernard's pass. One of us two will have long been mistaken, and on a matter so decisive. I can scarcely believe myself. I fumblingly find my way to the last quarter of an hour. And for my bewildered happiness, there I come upon the sublime fragment that has served as my magic horse for the duration of my forty years' reading – and thus sub-reading – the most adored of texts. Thus, say I to myself, gripped by a wondrous despondency, I have yet to read the book that I most love to read in the world, and which I have been reading ever since I began 'to read' in order to learn to read, studiously, obsessively, that is since year 1 of my Joycean era, date of my entry into reading life by death. I see it, it is not 'in the end' that he will have written 'In faith, I cannot go on, the subject surpasses the teller', but *all the time*. (I have just also noticed *for the first time*, after forty years, the presence, so delicious, so untranslatable of this 'in faith' – a formulation whose somewhat casual insistence in affirming upon faith the admission just made may well weaken the confession.)

The whole time he writes he writes surpassed, crawling along after the subject like a worm that the energy of desire drives to turn into a horse, ridiculous, unbelievable, the hand can no longer write, it is very cold, depicting that which he cannot depict, always in a forced margin

(I realize that I have never yet done one of the readings of *The Life of Henry Brulard* that I have long thought I should – a reading of all the margins of the book, or the marginalia, whose path runs the length of the main route. I have read a few, in order to speak about them, but for various reasons, of good or bad faith, I have not done it. Will I have read this column, in the end?)

To get back to my Joy upon entering the Box: the foregoing pages are a physical effect of this. The writing explodes, it
goes off in all directions in filaments of fire. As if fleeing the
too-great fire.

Escapes. I am searching for help. This Joy is beyond me. I
fear it will escape me. I want to hold it back. I want to bear witness to it, which is to say I should like to have witnesses to it.
Propagate it. Share its burn. Check its dimensions (Is it huge,
unique? Or something fairly harmless?) against the effect
that my discovery will have upon an interlocutor. I imagine
the suffocation in the chest of Richard Lepsius in 1842 at the
sight of the remains of remains of ruins slightly visible on the
east face of the mountain that enters him like a ball of fire in
the rib cage, I try to imagine the dreadful pain when he draws
out of the millennia's silence the telling-words, I imagine the
fear that knots the throat of Ludwig Borchardt at the idea that
perhaps his Joy will have been no more than a mirage without
echo in the desert of men. This has been known since Moses
the Egyptian, no sooner found than lost. There is none more
cast out by happiness than he who discovers its doorway. On
the one hand the subject surpasses the teller. On the other the
teller snuffs out the subject upon which he breathes. And yet
how can one not want to be surpassed?

The Box still somewhat given over to Secrecy. I could
have moved away. I still could. Throw this Box away without looking at it. Thrust the Subject down so deep into the
cupboard's throat that not a word will ever be spoken about
it again. There is still a little time. A little later I would start
to forget it. Later still I will have forgotten the forgetting. All
might yet be lost.

One more 1964 page that comes belatedly to me, to go either after page 53 or after page 57 and in any case before the book draws definitively away from Buffalo, which may happen – or not. I see myself retrospectively given over to the papers and manuscripts, and even devoted, I have taken holy orders and I haven't the heart for anything except Adonai, the Spirit who begets Literature. Nun. There is no other God but the God Literature and Joyce is his prophet, here is all that the Nun saw, she who *thinks* nothing, in a state of trance and floating of the body above the bookshelves of the library where she is.

§

I have great trouble now piecing together such a person who above all was absolutely not of this world and who, at this same time in 1964, had other existences of which I can find traces when I turn my attention to them. Existences led as if in a foreign country by a handful of foreign women. I had two or three years since entered into the immediately already unique and fateful famous friendship that I call the J. D. friendship, after the name of that greatest of geniuses, who was so obviously so in my eyes that before he wrote a line I had had the revelation in dreams of hundreds of brilliant volumes that he would go on to write in later years. It is to him, the greatest of all, that I later related all the incomprehensible events that crossed my path, *quite simply* – the raw, the dark, the menacing, whatever was secret from myself. Regularly, and without the need to account for these singularities ever becoming apparent to me. I think I can recall that in 1964 I would never think of him for months at a time, because the existence where I would meet with him regularly did not exist. In another existence I possessed an absolute happiness, all of whose features I recognized later in

Stendhalian passion: I was madly in love and was so loved in returned by Love itself. It is an experience of which I think rarely, without regret. I realize that that sentence is equivocal. I'll start again: it is an experience of which I think without regret, rarely, or else in which I think I participated without regret. I think without regret. I see that I cannot avoid regret. In truth there is nothing to regret. This happiness was the absolute each day, nourished by death and immortality, of the kind depicted by Stendhal, that poisons itself at its source. The subject could be of interest in another chapter. I believe – I don't swear to it – that on one occasion I was reproached for loving 'Joyce' more than him – to whom I shall here give the name 'Jean' –, which seems to me absurdly true. But it is the sign of, and something proper to, absolutelove to be persecuted by a jealousy of everything and nothing, since it is a passion that is jealous even of its own shadow. Besides, if I was literarily in love in 1964, it was with *Samson Agonistes*. I never felt for *Ulysses* the transports that a few cries from this Samson used to cause me. I can understand how one might fall madly in love with Bradamante. But I pictured Samson as a magnificent man with an eagle's brow, with vast and slightly soft muscles, and yet blind breasts on his chest. Whenever I heard him sounding out *o dark, dark, dark amid the blaze of noon*, I would experience a pleasure just as great as, but much sadder than, that caused me by a sigh from Heinrich – as I call Henry when we make love –, this cooing that is no longer that of a man but of a bird or a dying man in whom the soul is leaking away along with his sperm. And so I perch on the edge of the song, and I listen to this scansion, so poignant, this death rattle in the *a*, this more than human wail, *o dark dark dark*, these notes that escape all analysis, this groan of a god beaten by the strong solitude of pleasure *oh, ah, ah, ah*. True readers will understand.

If I had the time I would count up the number, some-how fated to finitude, of these existences. I'll cite only one more, for it re-appears in the Box – the one I led natu-rally as a threesome, with my children, an existence which has always followed me everywhere and whose trimitive, fleshly substance I reproduce with my cats. (I am reluc-tant to speak of that so lofty and ardent existence where I am with my father because its nature is other than all the others, as posthumous and perhaps superior in brilliance, in freedoms and intensities, to all, less constant and yet less vulnerable, and, in consideration for the other, the most tender, the most indulgent, the least subject to the wars and treacheries that beset even the most peaceable of our living existences.)

I envy the so clearly ordered structure of *The Odyssey*: for each locality an episode, and vice versa. Such a pleasant narrative navigation. A real sea voyage. That is what makes odysseys, however ferociously beaten by the elements they may be, as elegant as a whale – they follow the map. Whereas with me, I can see that what I am relating is overwhelmed by the irresistible attraction of the maelstrom that is hidden in the middle of the theatre, or thereabouts, under the carpet of the world: the episodes – and there are episodes – are snatched up by a monstrous force of attraction, they are borne along towards the abyss, suddenly some escape the mouth of the storm, though no one knows why and not for long. What is most strange is that once rejected, splintered, unmasted, run aground upon some shore, the story, once it has come to, finds itself on the same rock where it had broken its journey thirty years earlier. Naturally everything has changed on the surface but deep down absolutely nothing has changed. And so, a few days pass in 2009 as in 1964. The illu-sion holds the reality firmly, we live, love, weep, lose, protest, holding fast and fast in faith. Everything starts and re-starts in the same moment.

The Box has a force. It's odd. It won't be pushed around. I can't bring myself to go on as if I had not found it. There is a law. No one understands it. *When Mr Earnshaw finds the unnamable 'Subject' in one of Liverpool's streets, a law* obliges him not to leave him as he found him. He quite sees that he must take him home *at once*, in all his life, nothing will ever have so exhausted him, he casts himself down into an armchair, begging all around him without exception not to approach him for he is, so to speak, dead, as well as mortal and murderous. All around him are already lit up by the mortal emanations issuing of the Subject. The Subject has a power all his own. This power is stronger than those of all around him put together. What is striking is that the Subject, even as he is stationed in the middle of the study, is content to gaze around, seemingly astonished to be there, motionless, as if in truth he were not there, as if his sheath were set down in this place whilst his soul ran wild and uncoupled from reality in gypsy climes where oblivion, solitude and abandonment reign. He looks like a sleepwalker. From here on in, no one, nothing is incontestably sovereign. No one. Pure no one. An imposing presence.

It is as if there were an invisible steel thread between us, that is the illusion I have. I am bound. Was there perhaps a covenant? So long ago. A vanishing order? Or of conservation? A ghost, perhaps. And what if this were a case of a prodigal child?

Whom I almost called: the fore-keeper of the archives at the Bibliothèque Nationale de France. The woman super-institutionally appointed to that superlative title by J. D.

Everything I put down on paper, have already deposited and shall deposit, is somehow rightfully hers above all – a very curious pre-destiny and procedure which will lead me at some time or another to the necessity of commentary. The position she occupies or the position in my existence as pre-addressee and post-addressee of all that's lying around in boxes or out of boxes is such an oddity of fate that until now I have had neither the time nor the strength to consider it methodically. The presence of a fatality hanging over this situation inhibits my analytical verve. According to J. D. 'such a fore-keeper can only be 'bold and prophetic'. That goes without saying, he says. She knows, he says, the interminable and daunting task she assumes, he says, and that I, on the other hand, know not, or almost not, scarcely matters. I am no prophet but I am after the prophets.

And so I obey the first movement that presents itself within my ignorant and blind person, and threw myself like a child upon the telephone so as to declare the new session open. And there I stopped. Various obstacles halted my intention, I cannot remember exactly which, some, domestic, some dictated by the Resistances settled on a trivet in the unconscious. As a result I all but called on my fore-keeper. In the end I granted this allbutness pride of place in the chapter devoted to the addressees of the Story.

On 29 June I find my mother sitting in a large armchair, asleep. She is sleeping, her head downturned, her cane clutched in her hand. Alone in the room. I do not know what path she sleepwalks. 'Would you like to lie down, little mum?' 'No.' She says no without waking. Nothing will divert her from her path. After this scene I completely forget to call the fore-keeper.

No prophecy, I say to myself. I forget the Box. I no longer possess a single wish. I contemplate my mother's Wish: she *wants* to see her dream through to the end. What would I have said, had I not been diverted? I believe I would have shouted: 'I've found the manuscripts, the ones I hadn't lost.' I had always gone along with the hypothesis that they had been still-born, or spirited away by some mistakeeper and abandoned in the streets of Liverpool, worthless offspring, runts of a time that never grew up. I never went looking for them. They had not lived. I never felt regret. I did not dream of it. I remember that I remembered the faces of my first texts, I never forgot the notebooks with brown covers – small ones, in thick, sturdy skin, the pages sewn together, by which I held myself together nervously, trustingly. Since I imagined that they held half the power, they really did. I firmly propped myself up, I ran with conviction and nimbly, escorted and borne along by the tenacity of the volume, unfaltering, keeping a promise from one page to the next. The soul of the book in the making had the notebook's spirit – lean sturdy brusque square thick-set staunch. I did not stop on the point of falling with the left foot raised up the heel lifted the step measured the right foot pensive resting on one of the slabs unevenly lifted by the finger of an ancient pine root, I did not fight to hold back by the trimming of his robe a divinity who will have fled me for some years since never specified but very elevated, a life of years, I never received several warnings of immortality. It is true that I am sickly, strangely affected by my mother's incurable old age. I don't deny that the obscure and superhuman powers of the verdict have, upon all the parts of my being, unknown but perceptible and extremely distressing and disturbing effects. I sometimes think that it is perhaps my life-with-Ageing, that is in the service of Ageing, that brings about behavioural disturbances and which would explain (1) a certain number of auto-immune gestures. The fact that I

45

go up- and down- and back upstairs two or three times every hour and thus a good twenty times a day, to go and check that all is well in my mother's life, and that I perform these movements without waking externally so as to remain deep in my thoughts, all the while passing and re-passing the same twenty times in front of these cupboard doors, which may stir up the props. I notice that my cats constantly go up- and downstairs, and wrinkle the folds in their cats' lives, touched by the tides of distraction and anxiety; (2) even as I have swapped my traditional state of unmoving meditation for the coming-and-going overhaste of a spider assaulted by circumstances, I am also prey to implacable paralyses, I am spider and fly, I self-bind, I inject my venom into myself, I climb ladders on all eights, bare-legged, bitter-hearted and on the last rung suddenly turn into a fly with stupefied syrupy legs, and there I am my own captive and destined for self-devouring. At the foot of the ladder my mother and her cane squawk cries of frightened fledgelings, I let go of myself, I drop back down, I run to the nest, exhausted, clasping, I fly off again. And throughout this paradoxical escapade I clutch my crown and my thread between my teeth, I think only of writing later on, I'll write later on – Lateron is the gnome in the stairwell; (3) I am ageing and I set off backwards in the impotence of youth. To my great mortification, I am subjected by night to Tests of excellence or existence, able to do nothing about it, I am reevaluated by an invisible and anonymous tribunal that is none other than The Tribunal, and 'I finish' third, the best script is God's, I have it here before me, the first page flawless, white, but for the name GOD in big black elegant capitals. In the top left corner the ranking: first. I don't know who comes second and I'll never know. Perhaps that is for the best – I do not contest the rankings. Coming third is perhaps what Montesquieu will have said to Stendhal. One is modestified in truth. But what shames me is catching myself, and more than once, presenting myself before deliberative assemblies dressed in shorts, and only me too, and realizing that this is a serious error of judgment. On the one hand nothing reassures me that I haven't got bad legs. Were that the case I would be sure to attract unflattering remarks. Then I remember too late that one is much better advised to select clothing that covers the flesh, since it is the best way to stoke up desire.

I finally realize that these afflictions affecting my legs (paralysis, indecency, ridicule) are the result of a surreptitious introjection of the *tableau vivant*: my mother's legs. *Little fact to slip in*: like the bad smell of the people who attend vespers at the church where Henry Brulard, that is Henry Beyle, that is Stendhal, was taken – how do you paint a picture representing terrifying and repulsive lower limbs from the point of view of a subject whom leprosy and lesions make neither shudder nor recoil, repugnance being entirely inhibited and replaced by a naked sober neutral inexplicable love, as if humanely anaesthetized, all but infinite in extension since she extends her impassivity daily to a new pustule or a section of canvas that is scored and scaling like a burnt lizard? I cannot do it, and it is a source of regret, for there is within me a traveller who nurtures a sharp and passionate interest in such rare objects. This person, somewhat a painter but not enough, who stands just behind me, would like to make herself the Dante of a long descent into the desert of the Last Extremity. There are all but unbelievable experiences to be had there, so believed that you could all but believe yourself though you aren't in hallucination. You have to have been where you don't go naturally, move beyond lands discovered and baptized in ferocious Antarctic climes to draw closer to the time when you become uncharted. And yet in the daytime I do not side with the painter who awakens in me, come

47

the evening, when I proceed to mum's *Coucher.*[6] But the two spirits who plague me have a certain affinity. Mainly a *flair for folly*.

I say to myself: I started with the *First Extremity*. That was in 1964. By the end I will have entered the *Last Extremity*. Two evenly matched follies. The same twin.

I almost called the fore-keeper to tell her that I thought I'd found the ruins of the First Extremity, but then I didn't. As much as eleven or seventy years could go by between the moment when a passion lifts us from the earth to transport us to the land of chimeras and the day when we arrive at what will be called happiness (1800–11: Stendhal's case; 1842–1911: Lepsius's case; 1901–17: Shackleton's case)

Instead, I rang my son the astrophysicist. I try to pick out the circumstances surrounding the event. All conversations with my son are of a kind of astrality woven between us like a singular idiom. I turn to my son, the specialist of mysterious things that take place in the material sphere, in the heights as on and in the earth, and which hold no secrets for him. I did indeed find the Box about five minutes after he had left the house after spending twenty-four hours there. Why? During his stay the ongoing conversation was, as usual, about languages that are invented and one day stop being used. My son and I are in dialogue. Whenever I want to talk language I call my son. And it is as if it were Language who answered. Whenever we talk we talk language and languages.

---

[6] The *Coucher du roi* was the retiring ceremony of the King at the French court, which became a ceremonial custom under Louis XIV.

Over the decades that we have been telephonically weaving, we have openly built a monumental, complex, harmonious answering machine, with my son as the central switchboard, the brains, and me the workforce; my son is the wires and I the nimble fingers that weave and knot these extraordinarily fine threads. I sat down next to him, the Language-son. My mother sat down next to me. 'He's giving his course,' I cried. 'Coarse!' my mother cries. Three colours. Course, course and coarse. 'Four,' I cried. Course, course, coarse and corpse.

'*Pascal*,' says my son. Pascal is a language invented in the late sixties for pedagogical reasons. So that the theory of programming could be as close to the practice as possible. Things are spelt just as they are thought.

I'd like to learn Pascal but Pascal isn't used any more. The dessuscitation of Pascal. So there are languages spoken amongst ghosts. Or that are preserved in boxes. I believe I myself can remember having spoken a Pascal once. The name of this Pascal was Milton. Today, I am its last remaining speaker.

'*Camel*,' says my son. For a logo they used the camel from Camel, the cigarettes that no longer exist. Shadows, shadow language. Camel is a functional language.

Whilst I'm thinking of the story of the Box – a story made up of interweaving stories – that I do not yet know, I think of the story that my mother is now weaving from a language of flowers. It occurs to me that my mother is in the process of inventing a new language. She 'thinks' or elaborates with a flower program. What is a language? There are languages that are intermediaries between our language and machine language. Programming languages.

Geranium is the language with which my mother reads things as she 'sees' them, from her evolving viewpoint. 'Look,' says my mother, 'have you seen this flower? It's pretty.' I read: 'I am a geranium.' The accuracy of the statement fills me with admiration. She points a sharp finger: 'A wilted flower: there! Off!' I cut it off. I efface the wilting. 'Two texts,' says my son. 'A first text is a program,' says my son. 'Meaning a succession of commands to execute. A second text is the set of data upon which the commands are executed (images, music, text, geranium stems).' A text reads a text applies to a text. I read and I am read. I follow my mother to the letter. She commands me. I 'read': she gives me death and life, she orders me: 'bite'. I bite a piece of chocolate. She smiles. She hums. 'Simple, strong, I am the four colours of the Resurrection,' hums my mother's tongue. My mother is searching for a modern language – that is, one suited to her time, economical and analogical. There is a notable preference for the numbers three or four. I go looking for the Rosetta stone that will enable me to interpret this language. Things speak in the house, I say, mum talks to things, especially flowers. I have entered into telecommunication with the Box. I get an obscure sense that I am making anxious efforts to understand-guess-not-destroy-save-keep-gather frail, precious, vital messages sent out by essential sources – my mother the Box – on whom my whole future and history may depend.

'*Babbage*,' says my son. He *conceived* the machine to end all machines. The mother-machine and son-machine, the all-powerful, the infallible, the benevolent. And in the end he will never have seen it come to life. 'Babbage,' I say, 'is that a pseudonym?' 'Babbage is the first name of the machine-universe to compile the number-world. It is never wrong. Except that the author will never have lived to see his machine live.' I am Babbage. Thought Proust, thought I. We have the world. We conceive the language. We haven't time.

My son leaves. Enter the Box. My son has just left.

'The first real computer was mechanical,' says my son, 'and never worked because the precision mechanic to whom "Babbage" had entrusted the task of building the universal calculator was too slow in understanding the inventor's directions, as Babbage's long and painful correspondence with the mechanic testifies.' London's best mechanic also suffered endless hitches. No sooner had London's best mechanic almost finished making the eight thousand pieces of the *difference engine* than 'Babbage''s mental machine had once more pulled away, it grew more complicated as the mechanic honed, and as the inventor improved and modified it as a result. To this race against time must be added a supplementary difference conjoined to 'Babbage' in the person of 'Ada', Byron's daughter and the poet's double in all things – in genius, in fury, in poeticomathematical imagination. The *difference engine*, my son observes, was always a sexual – and at the same time, naturally, a textual – difference engine. Ada translates, adds, conceives, palindromatizes, brings the first mentally calculated and analytically incarnated child into the world; it is a memory that lives on today in its computational descendants. The names 'Ada' and 'Babbage' are obviously the vital parts in the mechanism of the difference engine which, at a few letters off the eight thousand characters, will have had neither the time nor the strength to see the light of day.

He had barely left when I turned towards cupboard A. It faced me, with its taunting, mechanical expression. I opened it. I gutted it like a chicken. An old chicken. I should have stopped there. There is no urgency or necessity to this emptying-out, it seems to me that it's the least of all urgencies. Something makes me move on to cupboard B.

51

℥

Since I arrived in the writing chest, where my primary concern ordinarily is to sit down at my desk to write, I have not been writing

I came here to write, thinking only of writing, or reading-for-writing, and since then I have not been writing, I say to myself, I still want to write but as soon as I sit down I get back up and turn, under hypnosis, towards the cupboards – the top ones then the bottom ones, I can't keep myself from *penning myself* into a compulsive activity that is entirely abnormal and surprising for someone like me who in forty years has not once gone in for such curettage, such revision. I have always been loath to use my time in this way; time must be devoted one hundred per cent to writing and I only deduct from this writing time what is vital for the survival of my mother and yet since the first day, truly racked by forces mainly hidden away in cupboards, I can't help but do away with forty years' worth of cupboard deposits in one fell swoop. I hear Voices. These inaudible but distinct grumblings that you can't shy away from since they sound within the cupboards and from there within my own intimate cupboards, my Heart, my Lungs, my Memory. It doesn't interest me at all, but everything has woken up. I cannot bear the cries. I open everything. I pull everything out. I don't understand any of it. And yet a friendly, gentle silence has reigned since 1966. Or so I thought. We were on the best of speaking terms. If there is *one* thing I really don't want to do it's exactly what I'm doing – clearing out cupboards, or giving in to the need to evacu-ate, purify, exorcize that I never feel. I am behaving with the same passivity that governs my adventures in dreams, I haul myself before these shelves, incapable of resistance, I exercise over myself the authority of impotence. I am a driver who's absent-mindedly taken her big car out for a spin, there's no going back, says my mother; I hope soon to reach a destination but there is no such thing, the boulevard goes on forever, it is Endless Boulevard, it is dark and I have time and darkness against me. It's at this moment that the big car slows down, the slowness gradually takes hold of the vehicle, no way to accelerate, I realize that there will be no more response and free-wheel gently, I was on Nighttime Boulevard now, I must have lost my way, I don't know this boulevard, this area is not in the city, and finally I settled myself gently against a deserted pavement, nowhere. I got out. I now had to call for help. I couldn't possibly say where I was. Phone? I'll phone my daughter, I say to myself, when I remember that she has another number in the other country. I began punching in the three numbers then stopped. 001. I saw a death sentence in this. Try as I might, my memory had broken down. There was a guy lying on a bench in front of the wardrobe. With a black bag. I'm going to recognize him. But I won't ever have been able to say what his name was. It's prohibited. I mistake it for mine – the bag, that is. And as consciousness returns to me, I set things straight and take mine. The guy is a maniac, a killer – I am careful not to say his name – but I react very vigorously by shouting: 'Get back! I'm calling the police right now.' But I know very well that there's no one I can call for help. I don't even have the number for the police. A fault on the line. Exactly – a write-off. Don't write.

§

Conversation with my son. Remains
(This exchange took place as if in a dream between two ages)

In the linen cupboard, I say to myself, a large, logically dusty box. What's the connection between the sheets and

the Box? Of which I knew nothing. Manuscripts I was sure I
had thrown out. We've never seen each other before in our
lives. That I cast out – into oblivion, only into oblivion. I put
forward the hypothesis that it's because you were there, I say
to my son. Because that's the only unusual element that I can
see. My son never gets to the house on the same day as me.
Something was out of synch, out of joint, or joined-up in the
house engine, one cog on one of the five thousand wheels
missing.

In the Box, the startling vision of photos so long forgotten, six of them, in postcard format. Six photos of Us, I say.
I meant to say photos of '*the family*', made up of the mother
with son and daughter, or the two children with mother that
we were, undivided, triunitarily. When I say 'We', it's that
number three of the family phylum that you can see here
captured on the photographic plates. A trefoil: Woman,
Daughter and Son. Those photos looked out at me as if I
were a stranger. It's true that I'm no longer that woman.
Whereas the children haven't changed. All of Us remains
in the gaze. It's the only element that got out alive from the
consignment to the shadows. So, I thought, there's that Us
kept hidden away like a manuscript amongst the manuscripts.
A light, I noted with surprised curiosity, has been cast upon
Us, produced no doubt by the artificial lighting of the studio,
which draws a distant glow and that envelopes Us in an allegorical halo. We've been doctored! I exclaimed. The light
from outside comes back and highlights the interior light
that flows from the six eyes with the unitarily naïve gaze.
Here is a portrait of Naivety. None of us has yet been hurt,
that much you can tell from the rounded unity of the flesh of
W, D and S. The characters are clearly prehistoric. I make a
note: it's because this phylum sits within the Box alongside
crime, terror, anxiety, melancholy, black clouds chained up

behind the lines of the manuscripts. Whereas the Trinity seems to know nothing of the trace. Just as within a funerary monument would be smiling a delicious depiction in brilliant colours of the joyful people the corpses once were. How long ago Us was! I say to myself. How docile, trusting, contented, ignorant, silly. The photographer has showered the backcloth with a dust like that of angels' wings. And yet that photo was definitely taken in 1965, at the height of my madness, at the famous pseudophilosophical time where I believe I remember that I believed everything that Friedrich Nietzsche believed himself to be, the stowaway son, who had secreted himself away in the house in all his clandestine glory. A season in hiding. In the photo, we look like philosophical lambs, tis pity, I say to myself, here are some figures as little aware of the existence of evil as the Alacalufes of the Tierra del Fuego were of the White Man's plague, and such figures with eyes like clear lakes call irresistibly for extermination. We were beasts before the fall and we did not know it. I would have liked to have called my daughter at the same time as my son just like in the photo, simultaneously, inseparably, but she had just left for North America, my day was her night.

Six photos of the mother with two children. The mother in the recommended pose – atop a very long turtle neck, a head *bowed* so as to keep one eye on the son and one on the daughter, in the manner, also favoured by the profession, of the classics of the genre. Madonna with her two children. The two children below are raising their eyes towards the mother's face. The trinitarian group smiles without suspecting that the murder of life awaits them behind the backcloth.

'It's your unusual presence, bearer of a high rate of childhood that has woken them up', I say. 'I'm sure you're right,' says my son, 'mum.' The word *mum* still fascinates us, it's a gem, as if we had kept a milk tooth. This can only be said in all modesty. I myself say *mum* to my son or daughter and we murmur Rimbaud in amongst the broom flowers between fables and seas.

Deferred conversation with my daughter

'Where?' 'On the floor.' Two boxes relegated side by side laid down. Sheets of life sheets of death. On the right the box laid down alongside the Box is full, heavy, nameless. Carefully shut. Flat memory. Look! I tell my daughter the secret of the second box – as I'm telling her, I realize that it's not that I had made nothing of it until now. On the contrary, no sooner had I opened the second box easily and almost with indifference than I had been all fired up, I had fled. I had shoved the second box away into the nearest past. Ah! That box was not yet extinguished. It is crammed with tins of Gourmet Gold cat food tins. No one would believe me but these little tins, each containing one hundred grams of food and which would fit in the palm of your hand, moved me as much as if, orphic, I had stretched out my fingers to brush the cheek of my cat Théa, the well beloved descended into the Underworld. The tins I was looking at were the ones, forgotten beneath the earth for thin, sharp years, that she would have eaten had she not been torn from me, in this very place, in the prime of our youth. Each of these tins, closed up on itself like a day that had been denied her after having been promised, remains, as a tiny funerary monument, an element of a commemorative installation. In 2002, when I finally have to let go of her body, having long fought for it against destruction, I kept everything that bore some relation to her: the hairs that from one day to the next had become strangely rare were gathered up wherever I had the unhappy fortune to find them, sometimes a hair had remained stuck on the edge of a notebook, others were cruelly few on the pillows. I was shaken – how a cat's

56

vestments can scatter and disappear as fast as the droplets of a wave. Naturally the shawl that was her veil, finery and shroud lies beyond all reach in the silk chest of my drawer. It seems to me that it is by the tins of cat food that I measured the infinite extent of the attachment. I loved Théa passionately. The use of the preterite is a mere concession that I force myself to make to bend to the pseudologic of acceptable feelings. The truth is that *I love her* with the raw love of a scorched heart. I fear the slightest 'sensible' remark. I keep my beloved sheltered from contact with so-called reality. I enjoy with her a heavenly and too brief happiness. (This is one place where I can use the resources of tenses to get away with staying in the present.) Besides, it's true that each day of happiness is heavenly, intangible, and finite. One morning at eleven o'clock, a delightful morning in late summer . . . My heart wants me not to *end* this sentence. I keep back for my own use the absolutely living memory of each hour that was silently working away at taking the adored one from me a little more. I have no distinct recollection of the cat food tins. The pain of that time absorbing all my strength and my thoughts, what I can say about it today, after the exhumation of the chest, is only a highly probable hypothesis. It will have been impossible for me to treat those tins like anonymous rubbish. I will have found it impossible to give them to anyone and from there will have had to admit that I won't be giving them to their intended recipient. I will also have found it impossible to give a poisoned gift, for I could not have avoided introducing deathly bitterness into the food. On the other hand I will have had to hide them so as to prevent some innocent, attentive hand from throwing them away after having checked their use-by date. These tins might have been savoured over the year that followed the beloved's leaving. I see the little columns of these tins like a miniaturized figure of the sublime Holocaust Memorial, whose two thousand

57

seven hundred and eleven stelae stand with irregular regularity as a field of mourning not far from the Brandenburg Gate in Berlin. This garden of sorrows is such a beautiful and mysterious grace that it gives you a taste of the strange sweetness of a well-seasoned grieving. You walk endlessly between the undulations of memory, remembering purely and with no precise memory, just the undulations. I walk amongst the piles of cat food tins and believe-I-hear the undulated call of the beloved. No one could dispute the profound bliss of the sadness aroused as you slip between the grilles, noiselessly, as if without knowing where to go, down the pathways that lead to the way back between the Brandenburg Gate and Potsdamer Platz. As I wandered peacefully between the rows, each differently similar, of memorial stelae that unsettle the bustle of the city and spread meditation, I thought I saw Théa threading her way to the corner of two pathways and waiting there for me to come and fetch her. In the same way, as I let my gaze thread its way through the grilles of the little columns of cat food I can feel the undulations of Berlin melancholy. Anyone might say that the concrete stelae do not move, and yet the field of two thousand seven hundred and eleven undulates like the spine of a cat. That can be verified. What is the state called 'remembering' if not the trembling raising of the immobile?

§

To the left of Théa's Memorial, there's a big, gagged box, I say to my daughter. On the side, scrawled in red felt-tip pen, the graffiti: *Jeffers/ Prénom/ de Dieu/ Ms/ Gr.* A collection of things happened fifty years ago. It's full of *old stuff*, I thought. How we deny ourselves. I open up to get rid. It's full of *young stuff*. I find myself having to forge a phrase up to mocking my own pre-judgements. This Box turns out to be youngest of

58

all, swelled with sap preserved like a sort of sperm entrusted
to a fairy sleep.

'You and cardboard boxes!' says my daughter.

As a general rule it is thought that a miracle only happens
once. But it's because we don't believe in miracles. We allow
destiny a whim, an accident. And yet a miracle by definition is
only a miracle if another miracle comes along to miracle-ize
it, to bring the event back to life, guarantee it a resurrection
as unpredictable naturally as the first dramatic occurrence.
The real miracle is anyway the fact that the miracle, which
is unique and can only happen once, should occur *contrary* to
all expectations, sweeping aside all our clichéd incredulities, a
second time. And yet you can naturally never *expect* a miracle
no. 2 – that goes without saying. But one of the blessed and
marvellous features of the miracle is precisely that it absorbs
us *in toto*, makes us a gift of the world and, fulfilling us, is
accompanied by no hope and no sensation of un-satisfaction.
Anything can happen and anything did happen. Thus, as my
daughter pointed out, I had already had a box filled with gold.
Fifteen years have gone by. The gold miracle has lost nothing
of its initial lustre. Its gleam detracts nothing from the radi-
ant uniqueness of the Box's resurfacing. In 1994, I say, it was
only a small box, worn and disquieting, whose gold I thought
for weeks that I had to refuse and if Arthur – as I called at the
time my friend the great poet when talking of his genius with
my daughter, the best Rimbaudphysicist – had not affirmed
and confirmed me in my right to the miracle I would never
have allowed myself to 'profit from chance'. You can't make
Literature out of gold, I said to myself, I can see myself looking at that little box with a sense of guilt, being made rich
overnight, without having deserved it, it is as if a masterpiece
had been written by 'me' whilst sleeping, and with no effort,

no deprivation of sky, of air, of movement, no long weeks mixing plaster and hammering at stone. I now know only one thing and that's that it was Henry, or rather Arthur, who rid me of my remorse-in-advance with no intervention from him – when it came to grace, he was there to receive it, with no fuss. 'Don't make a fuss,' he had said to me. Since I have never been able to *bear* the least hint of disapproval from Arthur, I say, to my daughter, a moment later I took the box and it was fine. I still don't know why I kicked up such a fuss. In a sense, I thought, talking about it to my daughter, the upshot is that it was as if Henry had given me what I found. But my torments remained above suspicion. In conclusion, I said to my daughter, one cannot *find* anything – one can only receive and be blessed, and that requires the soul to kneel into childhood and to miaow for help from a 'mum'.

The first time we *saw* Nofretete in Berlin, together, I say to my daughter, it was *the same thing*. It was in 1984 but it was perhaps in 1988, I say. It was the first time and it wasn't the first time, you know? I say. (I always say 'you know?' to my daughter when I *know*, and *because* I know, that she knows, whereas the one who is not sure she 'knows' what I am groping for between my thoughts is me. And I was trying to shore up my path by propping it up with my vital acolyte. If she understands then I am not definitively lost in my shadows.) For me it was the first time that I was seeing Nofretete *in reality*, I say. I had already seen her dozens of times perhaps hundreds, in photos, in dreams, on postcards, I had received postcards called Nofretete, where you could see her from the front, from the back, from one profile to the other, three-quarters on, so never whole, always from an angle, bathed in such an artificial light as to give her an allegorical halo, these cards are sent to me sometimes by friends, sometimes by strangers, sometimes by Henry, and in that case the gift is set apart from the others by the fact that he always sends me more than one postcard in the same envelope or else a card with several views of Nofretete – I should count them one day, I say, up until now not only have I not done so, I feel like I have *discarded* these cards, like I have wilfully discarded and mislaid them. To come back to Berlin, when I say that I saw her in reality it's a manner of speaking, as is 'for the first time', a manner of speaking, but there is an element of truth to it. It really was the first time that I saw her in Berlin, in all her dimensions, from all her angles, it was Arthur, as I call him, who had taken me there, and it is this company and this immense and silent commentary that he is that constituted 'the first time' in its entirety. For him, it was not the first time that he came to see her. But it was the first time, that much was plain to see. I saw a surprise spread like sunburn across his face. I was surprised. I remember him talking to himself: 'I would never have thought . . .,' he said, I can still remember this clearly to this day, in the murmur demanded by the museum there rang out a mixed note, an infinite complication of sadness rapt by the surprise of having surely survived a death, a note of fearful and sad joy, sad for having survived rapt at having survived a death but gripped in that same moment by a regret to come, by a presentiment of never again, as if there were the strange sorrow for having lost a death mixed with the frightened relief at finding himself alive after the end. 'You know?' 'I think so', my daughter murmurs. 'And the end of the sentence?' 'I think,' I say, that it was '*I would find myself back here.*' Or '*find myself back here with you.*' But all the undulated passion was in the first part of the statement. There was of course no 'reality' in the room. What is beautiful, I say to my daughter, is the *unutterable* materiality of Nofretete. Everyone who sees her thinks she looks absolutely 'alive'. Much more real and alive than those who come to look at her and who variously fidget before her

61

frankly indifferent pose. And yet everyone thinks she looks so 'real' that it's as if she were a cardboard cut-out. Such perfection in the appearance of truth can only be achieved if the flesh is fashioned from the most accommodating, the lightest, the strongest and the most sublimatable material, which is cardboard. Besides, no one has ever accepted without resistance this incomprehensible existence that nothing stalls and which is perpetuated by this name Nofretete. But when my friend Henry, who was, however, the greatest poet, said 'So I will have re-visited her,' I heard perfectly that it wasn't the existence of Nofretete that seems to him to surpass reality and reason – it is his. He himself, Arthur, I say to my daughter, has trouble believing that he exists. It is as if the original were too beautiful, you know? I don't.

To come back to the Box, I would never have thought that I would see it again, I could not even have regretted the impossibility for me of ever seeing it again, I have lived for forty years four metres away from this Object and I was able not to sense the least intimation of its presence! There never was any presence. I open the cupboard around three thousand times, there is also the broom that I slip in just in front of the shelves behind the doors and I don't feel anything. I don't say anything to myself. In Paris, though, there are boxes in a cubbyhole that contain *things*. I hurry past them with downturned eyes, I avoid them, I ignore them, I acknowledge them negatively, I cross them out I don't answer. The Box will have been the Stele of Absence. I see that it could have ended up in the rubbish. I could have said to my brother: how about clearing out that cupboard? A bin. I could cry the tears that I would never have shed. And the cupboard! A sacred – or more or less – wood is what it has become to me. I did think about ripping it out last year. I dreamt about tearing down the dividing walls between the two rooms that formed its shelter, but then I pushed it out of my mind.

'You and cardboard boxes,' countersigns my Daughter. 'Something in the air made me find the Box. A spell,' I say. I want to think it's Us that put pressure on my memory. It is said that icons have certain powers.

URGENT. ENDURANCE 1

In the place where I talk Boxes incessantly whilst on the floor above my mother as soon as I approach to talk geraniums cries: *Fourcolours*, on 12 July where I realize that somewhere in the streets of Forgetting she has lost her 'Mrs Box' tune, I suddenly slip in the chapter that I had entitled 'Repetition', or 'My mother packs her boxes'. This is urgent – in this scene my mother will be seen demonstrating her cardboard boxing skills: lightweight, strong, supple, going about her business – all this a month ago – as she no longer could; here, then, on this page, so as to stay once again as close as possible to a realistic time sequence. We are *flying* through our time, my mother and I – it's enough to make the head spin. As we make our way along at a speed that's beyond me, in the time next door I go slowly back up, almost meandering, with the unconscious prodigality of those who have yet to experience the sudden brevity of time, a blubbery, hot, ample, sky-blue time that I share out equally with my two children on both sides of my childhood. A slow-time nonchalant and creamy, a time of milk and cows, ruminating, thick, apparently inexhaustible. The other one, in the same stairwell, takes flight. It's a precise flight, a crumbling away where each day turns up new damage. Here's the scene – become ancient in two weeks – like the whistle of a missed train – won't be back – still time to rescue the comedy rating? A ratio calculated to the power of my mother from a time so near so far where she packed a box – which I did not know at the time was probably the last possible. And yet it was 25 June of this year of bubble-wrapped months. So the box is the one that my mother packed the day before we left Paris – a head-spinning day it was. In this 'dream', Mrs Bo., a big fat woman, more or less square in all directions, very professional she is, arrives, with armfuls of headstones. The square table. My mother's with me, in A. I am impressed. Mustn't this woman have hidden strength to carry all these headstones, which, smaller than usual maybe, are nonetheless in marble and granite. Headstones now on the table. Mrs Bo. in B. Your own cemetery straight to your door. Box and Yew. Funeral Directors. Excellent choice. I ask myself whether this scene is real. My cat, lying on the headstones, seems 'real'. Leaving aside our affected affects. Mrs Bo., leading: 'What would you like?' My mother mis-leading: 'A plain coffin, unlined.' Mrs Bo.: 'What do you call plain?' My mother: '*The plainest*.' Mrs Bo: 'Champagne? White?' My mother: 'No.' Adds: 'No champagne, no white.' Mrs Bo.: 'No can do. Lining compulsory.' My mother: 'Why lining? No need.' Mrs Bo.: 'It's the law.' My mother: 'No frills.' Mrs Bo.: 'On the coffin?' My mother: '*Plain as can be*.' Mrs Bo.: 'It's compulsory.' My mother: 'No one's pinching my coffin.' Mrs Bo., nervous, pushes a headstone: 'In oak or pine?' My mother: 'Do I know the difference?' Mrs Bo.: 'Hard, less hard.' My mother, hard: 'I'd rather a soft wood and di-sa-ppear-qui-ck-ly.' Thinks: if only you could bury yourself. Everyone burying themselves as they liked. Mrs Bo.: 'Are

66

these to your satisfaction? They're nut-covers.' My mother: 'What for? *I'm not.*' Mrs Bo.: 'Looks better. When you close the coffin, always nuts.' My mother: 'I'm not nuts. I'm not after some out-of-this-world coffin. No nut-covers. What's the point? Covering things up? (*Pause.*) Point's to disappear. Best have pine.' Mrs Bo., hammers in a nail: 'Will you be passing away at home?' And my mother's surviving, I say to myself. 'With or without rabbi?' 'Rabbinimum.' 'Taharah?' 'My daughter will be helping me.' Mrs Bo., dismayed, sitting on a headstone: 'Would you like to be buried in a shroud?' *(Here, in the corner of this paragraph, inspired, my mother is help-ing me – my current mother comes out of the bathroom, her hair dripping. 'Dry me.' I dry her hair. The locks of hair spread out, all frizzy. I wrap her body in a bathrobe. I slip her feet into swimming pool blue slippers.)* Mrs Bo.: 'Flowers?' This time Mrs Bo. has something over her. My mother hesitates. Mrs Bo., nascent triumph: 'Well? Flowers?' My mother turns her face towards the face of Daughter. What should I think? say her eyes. I hesitate. This year my mother has sided with *geraniums* over 'reality'. I hear in the bee-like buzzing of her hesitation the fact that she cannot give up her flowers, objectively, the gera-niums are cats that never leave, the language of geraniums is strong, modest, colourful, without violence, geraniums are also somehow vegetables which are easily prepared; she can peel them without effort, whereas other vegetables require the strain of movement that she can no longer afford. So I say: 'You like flowers.' So she says: 'We won't stop them bringing flowers.' So we say: 'Geraniums, we'll bring them.' Mrs Bo.: 'No roses then?' I say: 'No, no roses. That's all.' 'No, it's not all,' says Mrs Bo. She pushes a headstone towards us. Something in the papers? *Le Monde* or *Le Figaro*? Battle has recommenced. This time the climate changes from one minute to the next. A backhanded strike from my mother: 'M'not famous. And I've had time to be forgotten.' 'A visitor book?' 'What kind of rubbish is that? Just try to keep people away, mydaughter. Just thinking about it gets my back up. You turn into a vegetable. Needs to rot down quick. Mydaughter will take care of the geraniums. You have to make space for other people. *I've got my boxes packed*. Everyone should *pack their boxes* without a fuss.' Suddenly I see my mother get up (this was a fortnight ago) to push Mrs Box, who *seems* to want to attack her, briskly pick up a worn straw hat and hold it in front of her like a shield. The next part is a blank. Then I find us making our getaway, the both of us in the very old white car that is my mother's metal twin sister. A sort of white geranium on wheels that my mother admires as one of her own, and a hint of jealousy as the car still works. But it's my mother who's driving. Which is the same as saying that the impossible is happening. And of course I go along with this. It's tiring. The old girl has had it. One can't say she's running – she's crawling along, but fast, like a wounded field mouse or a crazy reptile, and making a clunking sound that I can only notice and keep my terror to myself. Obedience to necessity. I am well trained. The boulevard that we are crawling up on a sharp incline looks exactly like Boulevard Bru, the boulevard that leads to the Algiers Cemetery. Maybe that's why there is not a soul on this wide thoroughfare. She hasn't been of this world for some time now. But when my mother, at the fork in the world, turns the old girl off onto the no-entry slip-road that leads to the precipice I object. Haven't we just signed the papers for the 'life insurance'? 'Stop,' I shouted – in vain, because my mother cannot brake. 'Stop,' I shouted, I shout three times 'Brake! Brake! Stop!' She doesn't hear me. I can already see the abyss. I yell I strike a violent blow of a scream at the dream's membrane. It's the last minute. It was the last minute.

'I drove well, didn't I?' says my mother. Sheepish. Quite pleased. 'Very well,' I say.

Evidence of the effect of this Box amongst my sometimes sad ruminations.

Certain phrases roll heavy like blocks of marble. The cat, a black Japanese brushstroke – a Hiroshige – on the headstones. I don't know now whether we are in the dream when Mrs Bo. collects up the pile of headstones or whether we are out of it. You can feel the opposition between the fine, black leap of the cat and the inertia of the funerary pawns. Mrs Bo. says: 'When I see a cat as a simple manifestation of the nature of life, I regret not being lucky enough to have a cat – my husband's allergic.' Either the husband or the cat. Mrs Bo. concludes: '*I will get a cat in the end*, because men die younger than women.' Then everyone has a vodka. My mother cites Schopenhauer. She has never read him. I interpret this as a secret and desperate way of invoking Arthur. So it is a dream. Some of it, at least.

We come over a little lightheaded for having survived. After all, my mother has packed her boxes and we have come through it alive.
'I think I could still drive,' says my mother. 'Through the mouth. Give advice. Beautiful these flowers. Four colours! Ha! Ha!' 'Yes,' I say. 'Move this chair! Want to see 'em all! Four *different* colours.' In the end it's just colour. It's the beauty of the colour of differences. It's not the same pink. Differences are beauty.

At the end of the first week of confusion, I revolt against what I believe to be the verdict of reality. I decide to consult my old, out of use Pythia. I'll ask her: should I unearth what's hidden away in this Box? Of course I do know the limits of her 2009 wisdom, I say to myself. I remember that I caught her yesterday bragging about the unimaginable greatness of her age, in front of visitors impressed by the splendour that continuous consumption of cortisone gives her. '96!' she boasted. '96! 96!' cry the two enthused visitors. '96! Ha! Ha!' laughs my mother, laughing at the top of her voice, '96!' She said that as she would have said 106, or even two thousand seven hundred and eleven! She can't believe it! And just as she would have shouted 'Himalayas!' 'Bravo! Bravo!' shout the two cameramen! 'Not 96! Not 96!' I say, '99!' At that moment I was following a ridiculously realistic logic. No one heard me: I was spared the ridicule of having 'corrected' my mother's age, and therefore my mother, and the number 96, as if that made any difference at all. I have time exactly where I want it, I say to myself. I thought myself disabused of my philosophical fantasies. The day when my mother had just invented another wisdom. Who knows? I said to myself. She might have discovered a machine to turn back time. She has found a way to un-age. 'What about me,' I say, 'how old am I then?' 'Oh! I'd rather not think about that!' She stops laughing. Cautious: 'Who knows, you could even be 70?' This hypothesis floored her, I assured her that I wasn't there yet, no, no, she could safely rely on her 96 years, all that is beyond representation. She sees so clearly, I say to myself. In my nocturnal travels I myself often hover around 40 or 50, though I never look it – 50 or 35, depending. In certain dreams, that is for a big part of my life, at least 40 per cent of the time I have so far been in my early forties. My friend Arthur, that is Henry, was never inwardly more than 35, he told me, when we were making love, in reality, so exactly as if in a dream, and I can also remember the indescribable astonishment of the other Henry – Brulard – repeating to himself 'I am going to be 50 though in 1836 I have quite the same score of years as in the first flush of happiness.' What fictions we are, I say to myself. There I was thinking she was around a hundred!

She's giving herself time, all the time, I say to myself. A sovereignty.

'So you're 96?' 'Yesh.' Tell me, I find these flowers extraordinary – four colours of the same kind. I am just admiring the fourcolours and behind there is yet another colour.

I ask the Pythia: 'Should I take a look around the Box?' 'Why not?'

She has given her verdict: look on the bright side.

The Box is full of time. What is in the Box: a cube of time, carved up into the matter-history of my life, and structured like corrugated cardboard: two sheets of paper, with a third sheet – also corrugated – in between. There is no more wonderfully durable material than paper time. In the Box, the main characters are not yet 30, apart from Jeffers. They are the average tragic age – between 16 and 35, sometimes 16, sometimes 27, sometimes 35 depending on scene and type. They stay the course, these mythological warriors in paper armour stood upright beneath the gothic vault of the passing years. Because the pressure exerted by the force of oblivion follows the lines of the vault, the inhabitants of the Box are well protected. I am fascinated by the textual properties of life on paper, by the fact that memory has found a way to protect itself and to protect the youth of its characters in the folds of a fabric!

It is now almost three weeks since I opened cupboard B. Immediately afterwards I opened the Box. I checked its contents. I noted the presence of the manuscripts of a certain number of stories in a volume with which I myself was unacquainted. Not only was I totally and involuntarily ignorant of the existence of these manuscripts, I also quite as totally, and yet obstinately and voluntarily, refused to *read* this book, and so out of caution, so as to avoid being driven to 'read' it – that is, this book – I inadvertently never had a copy under my roof. I do not know when I began not-reading it. I was no doubt not so firm in my *decision* never to read it when it all began. At first one rejects by reflex, then comes organized resistance.

I have entirely forgotten the circumstances and the moments of conception of these texts.

My feeling is that it was already the time when 'the book', which was not and never was for me *a* book, 'an' individual, with a book-like, nor even bookish purpose, which is to say more precisely the various elements of the whole, the wheels of the *delibrium* machine, were produced, always in the dark, it was at that time, during the *uncertain-times*, which always wandered through the most foreign and disturbing regions of this internal country that we wrongly call 'past' although it keeps up its undesirable vagabondage in our heartlands of today, its little claws firmly dug into our arms and our ankles or in the seat of our armchair, it was then, when these *things*, these stages of being, these caterpillars, these larvae somehow found their way into my sheets, under my haunted pillows – in tumult at the back of my neck, it has to be said –, took on life, took on form in the shape of letters squirming on sheets of paper intended for my thesis notes, it is probably already at that time by a sort of repulsive gestation that, in all probability, I must have been weaned off any idea, all desire ever to 'read', and thus squarely to face, yes, to stare at these masks. I have entirely forgotten the true material circumstances of the appearance of these 'things', I cannot remember the days, the props, the desires, the places, tables, benches, cities, countries, whether they manifested, slithered, murmured in California, in Algeria, in Manhattan, Athens, Stockholm, in a port, I can nowhere see myself meeting them, waiting for them, or on a ferry, in an airport crowd. Whereas for *the book* that *I wrote*, I was perfectly present for months, at different times, spread out across time and space. I can see myself sitting on a jetty in the port of Algiers to write down the first sentences of the prologue for *Inside*, which I named without hesitation months later. This time, I am unusually on a bench at the famous Hôtel Saint-Georges, I can still see the bench enveloped by bougainvilleas and laurel bushes, I can see that I am wearing a dress – I cannot see precisely which one but if I really tried I could –, and it is one of those balmily sunlit days that bring blue winds and the births of books and bliss in incest, blessed by the gods.

Once the publication of the *unread* was complete, naturally not through my attentions but through the caring and kindly attentions of my friend J. D., it was as if it finally no longer had any hold upon me. Never again will it have any power over me, I thought. It has been everywhere I went for a year or two, and now it is nowhere anymore. I owe this purification to J. D. There had been demonic swine in the house and the house had now been disenchanted. That was what I thought. Naturally I kept from saying a word about it and later from thinking about it. One cannot say: I deny you. It's as good as blowing on embers. You have to simulate indifference and feel it. It is an inside-out prayer. There are such savages rising up from tombs, and suddenly someone comes along unperturbed and says: Come now. And all of a sudden they lie down into a book. That is how it happened. 'Come now!' said J. D.

As I ran off, he pressed on. It was not a book. For me it was a wild herd of larvae writhing weakly at the foot of my bed, I hurriedly took out a pad of paper and put it between me and the masks, as a precarious shield. Then I threw the pad away from me, in a terrified haste, my hands shaking – the paper clearly bore the marks of the larvae's tracks, and it was a vulgar trampling. But for him, J. D., it was definitely a 'book'. In 1964 or 1965, I don't recall ever having told him how repulsive the herd was to me, since the persecution was clearly aimed at me, and not him. Besides, I never talk about the purulence of my internal plagues, I keep my diseases a secret, I cloak them in the appearance of strength and health, I have always placed fourflowers in front of my stage just as my mother now arranges trailing geraniums before the enormous cavity of her old age. If for him the things were, in the end, a book, on the one hand I did not doubt it, on the other that by no means kept them from giving me the shivers. What the publication of the things brought me was a lessening of my fear: with the larvae bound and locked up in a cardboard cage I no longer felt as if the snakelions were roaming around my house, *unleashed*. Once it was published, or caught and removed, I undertook to forget about it. And I totally forgot about it. (Immediately I started 'writing' without running away.) It had become the-Book-that-I-don't-know.

How wrong we are when we *mean* to tell the truth. And I do want to tell to truth.

THE NAMELESS BOOK

By now the-Book-that-could-never-be-read escorted my mind, followed me everywhere in the sweltering forest of my thoughts, hounded me, entered my study, never left my side. I could see it very distinctly, nothing was more familiar to me than its little pale yellow face. I do not know whether I am unintentionally calling to it and whether it is responding to my nervousness, my fears, or whether it is driven to persecute me by an inner demon, but it is there, an unmistakable, indubitable spectre. I think of it or it thinks of me, as soon as I go from dreaming to thinking, at the start of dawn, it is already in the corridor, if truth be told it alreadyis, the word *already* is its password, I suspect that this word that greets it as soon as I move towards waking is its secret name, and it waits for me. I find it lain down on its side at the foot of the bed, crouched behind the bathroom door – I thought it might let go of me whilst I was in the shower but then it slips behind my forehead. I follow it, on the stairs it flies down one step ahead of me. I can more or less make out its features. I recognize it: one of the signs of my ancient resistance to its – always spectral – insistence is the forgetting of its exact name. As in cases of half-forgetting of names, a slight confusion has always held all knowledge of its name at bay. I secretly resigned myself to it, then grew accustomed, obscurely sensing that my hesitation came from it, from its being turned back in on itself, from its hesitation on the brink of being, denizen of the depths of the abyss that it is, abyssal scavenger from the time when it was not yet born. Of all of them, it is the only one of my books that always seemed to loiter, preferably in stairwells, trailing with it a certain number of fantasmatic but tenacious apprehensions. I associate it with tragic falls, I see it and miss a step, and the fall breaks not only my limbs but the child that at that moment I am carrying in my arms – a little boy – and since the accident or the incident happens again, as if I could not go down the stairs that lead from my study to the ground without falling, without being preceded in the stairwell by this horror-filled scenario, I ended up telling myself that the little one that I take with me in my fall (which naturally unleashes such a dreadful guilty affect that I cannot acknowledge it at all) is perhaps after all, it, none other, the Book that I 'made' and which I don't want. But did I 'make' it? For me, 'someone' put it there. And it's this inaugural and mysterious violence that will have caused so many incalculable after-effects in my life of being and in the other one, the substitute life, or substitute's life, this life that I spend killing the other life, the apparent and real one, in order to lead it, the real life, on fabulous nights that I prowl around in even in full daylight.

I have never really 'known' or managed to find out what the Book's real name was, although you couldn't say that I have forgotten it. I straight away not-knew. I myself did not name it. Didn't give a name. Not giving a name to someone always has nefarious consequences even if there are consequences that can be felicitous. Don't give a name to a cat that's none-theless taking refuge with you and food and affection, and at the end of the month it will die, it will have committed suicide, carrying out that which you did not want to recognize that you wished for without really wanting it: that it had never been. For a newborn two days, one day even, without a name is enough for the seventy years afterwards not to erase the trace of the nay where the name should have been, the insatiable fury of the abandoned child. As for the Book, if it wanders and as a result if it so happens that I wander in speaking of it, it is not for lack of greeting upon its birth with a sort of name that awaited it as the Night withdrew from It by leav-ing it at the edge of a half-day. No. The Book was recognized and called. Enthroned. Blessed perhaps, but I was not there, but I do not remember the moment when it was presented to me, as coming back to me from whence it came, returned, crowned I had thought perhaps or perhaps graduated, having passed the test of the examination in entering the people. There never was a memory. I always referred to it doubtfully – approximately is the word. As you hesitate with modesty and embarrassment when pronouncing the name of someone foreign whom one knows by instinct, in fear of getting some-thing out-of-place, of causing a confusion. And so, when I say 'I am looking for Le Prénom de Dieu' I am quite prepared to be corrected. The Book is called something like that. For me, it really is 'Something like that'. The Book is called something to do with first name, or names. I am not ashamed to admit that I have gone so far as to consult the 'by the same author' index that comes with my other books, but to no avail: some-times the book is called *Le Prénom de Dieu*, sometimes *Prénom de Dieu*, sometimes *Prénoms de Dieu*. That changes everything, everything is nothing, everything is God, only God remains, invariable Remains of everything. So much for the archive, the science of history, the reliability of memory. Of all of them, it is the singularity and privilege of this Book to have a floating name. It has been known for me to stammer as I refer to it, to fall back on some antonomasia or other. I'll say: the floating Book. Or the Book before my books. Or the less-Book. Or the Book that I shall never know. Whatever I do or don't know about it. Sometimes, when out, I'll say: 'the Book that J.D. talked about so particularly in his book.' His favourite.

Here I'll say: just as there are two M. de Charluses, there are two books by the name of *Le Prénom de Dieu* (or *prénoms*, depending): the one that J.D. read. And the one that I have not read. I am convinced that these two books – kept one inside the other within the same volume – are totally different. But naturally the fact that the same Book, which I myself shudderingly dismiss and shun, should have been at the same time received without hostility and treated with generosity and interest by J.D. adds an immense and complex added-value to this same Book, which I could peacefully detest were it not placed under the protection of my friend. This very old and perhaps even inaugural discordancy, and which was also the only one of its type in the long duration of the friendship, calls for an explanation. I'll give it some thought.

The fact that such a 'name' or 'title' should be floating might be due to my original disquiet. But when it comes to 'God', one might also expect attempts to approach a title proper to *Him* to fall back down, shattered in advance beneath the harpoons that wish to strike the Celestial Whale. Another hypothesis: suppose that the 'author' had dreamt about writing a book starting with such a title, entitled by God's entitlements, suppose that the title *preceded* the book and so God too, and that from the outset it was its undoing. I say all that not on my own behalf.

Either the Title will have preceded, or it will have followed. If the latter it could be said that God's first name is the whole lot of all the words, all the letters, all the signs and phrases penned into the enclosure that is the book. I imagine: mooing-lowing-hissing-cawing-murmuring-whimpering-trilling-panting from the flock of the text, its music clinging together in a floodtide of the French language.

ℬ

The Last Extremity

Yesterday morning (19 July 2009) I find my mother *deep* in her book on the *Endurance*, as if hypnotized – she is reading heavily weighs dips in ten, maybe dozens of times every line or perhaps between the lines, scrapes at the furrow, burrows, without lifting her eyes, holds the paper firm, the page, passes a bend, catches her breath without taking her eyes off the track, sighs very deeply, sets back off, something drags, wades on, no, retraces her words, a drift no doubt, then back at the start of the path, decides to press on, further ahead, without let-up, goes on step by step along the page, I can see her working, speculating, sizing up, taking a decision around midday she goes back, quickly, this time to the opening lines, either some fardel or sense has fallen away, or else she must have had her doubts about how far the page might take her. When I lean in to see where she has got to, I notice that she has come back to the morning of '21 April' on Elephant Island on page 171, the days spent gathering together frozen canvases laths sledge-runners box-lids used to invent a makeshift 'raft' to make the impossible crossing of the sub-Antarctic ocean, so just before the storm of 23 April and sixteen days before the page within sight of Patience Camp on the other side of death, in South Georgia.

The following day, 20 July, she went back to 2 April. Deep are the valleys between the towering waves, high the pages like mountains when she perches, her nose sharpened by the effort so as to see the pack lines peep through, momentarily atop a giant crest. I discover that she has stopped reading the pages in order. That gets you nowhere. She makes it through a good ten pages tugging her thoughts behind her. And from one line to the next the track is carried away by a wave as white as wool. Although perhaps she has chosen to turn the clock back to 1914 or maybe 1913. 1913, a year when death had not yet reached her ship. Will she have read it, in the end, the *Endurance*, how will she have 'read' it, what is it to 'read' the *Endurance*? I say to myself. Maybe she is in the process of re-doubling the *Endurance*, she will have found a way to make it last, perhaps she is trying to put off the ending, but maybe it is the same with all books, as long as the book lasts, right now she is on page 154. She stays there for a few days. On 1 August I shall decide to give her Edmondo de Amicis's *On Blue Water* to read. I had read Amicis's books as a child, I had forgotten them. When the month is almost out I realize that all the books I suggest to my mother this season are set at *The Last Extremity*. All the characters in these books are *passengers*. They are all determined to reach the Last Extremity and from 'there' to go beyond and from one beyond to an Other. They employ all methods of transportation, especially the least suitable, the most crumbling, ramshackle rowboats, cardboard yachts, trains driven by fine old bus-drivers through valleys as narrow as guts where railways are drowned in torrents of yellowish water, their supplies are laughable – plastic bags with an orange juice in, they are off to the End of the World, and they think the world has an End, but it's often the name that draws them and carries them. The *Last Extremity*, the *Endurance*, the *End of the World*, names of those old ships – faithful, proud, a little foolhardy, buildings made of paper and wills. We are aboard the ship that has departed the century and is navigating towards the Unknown. Awful these regions are, says my mother. They have been to terrifying places and they are not afraid of dying. When they are young they don't care. But I am no adventurer. I was. I went to Lisbon with Eri at 70 imagine that. '90,' I say. 'In any case,' says my mother, who all of a sudden went from 90 back to 70, 'we were no youngsters.' The ship is heading towards regions of which we have no representation. The Faraway Continent, our destination, is a jumble of illusions and ignorances. None of the passengers is happy. Everyone feels as if they are four years old again and have lost their mum. Four years old minus mum is dreadful. The feeling that dominates these souls is the poignant melancholy of being-abandoned. It is the most universal and primitive of anxieties: waking up from one's nap all alone in the world, with Solitude for pale company. Saying that, I can feel that that pain, the *unhappiest* of pains, has reached me. Our supplies are getting low. Mum is getting low, I say to myself.

I am reading more and more. She is rationing herself.

'One only reads at the last extremity.' My friend Henry had said that, exactly a year ago to the day. I did not believe him: wasn't he reading at the time? I thought. And what? Someone else's memoirs. He recommended the memoirs to me. Here, you've probably read the *Memoirs of the Comtesse de Boigne*. A book for invalids, he said. Or else as soon as one reads these memoirs, or memoirs in general, one immediately finds oneself at the last extremity. I did not understand all of that phrase. That's the hallmark of our friendship: I am never sure I have understood what he's getting at. Or else, as a perpetual reader he will always have been at the Last Extremity.

At this point it occurs to me that the only time, the only occasion when I could 'read' this book with the floating title, could only be in truth at the Last Extremity if I knew when that was. But according to Henry, the Last Extremity is all the time, whenever you like, the moment you read for want of living, as soon as you start reading you are already outside yourself, *en route* for the superlative, outside, and so heading off in the direction of the outermost outside. I look around my little writing room – a cube lined with two thousand volumes that form a coat an internal skin a uterine library, my innermost, my Chinese armour. It's true that as soon as I find myself there I stay Out-There. Two thousand extremities, fifty to a shelf. And that is nothing. I have never known anyone take in as many books as Henry. They are no longer books, they're cockroaches. They are everywhere, slow, noiseless, immemorial. Not only has he been forced to expand his bookshelves, on which his own works, as many as they are, only take up a double shelf, but he is driven to buy books, he cannot help himself, he cannot not leave the house without buying a few books, you can sense that he is *on the lookout* and I have come to think that perhaps that is the last extremity. Sometimes he buys me a book. I try to work out the intention. It is always a book that I would not have bought. A book that does not figure in my inner cargo. A stranger. Naturally it contains a secret, my friend always sends me secrets. In some cases I end up thinking that the whole secret is there in such-and-such a title. In some cases I still haven't worked it out. At that moment, I remember that sentence I did not believe in, maybe I would understand it now, maybe I have somehow started to hear the echoing of its depths. Of all the people I've known, he's the one who has always bought the most books. Enough to build a cathedral. A hundred times more than me. I buy two books, he buys two hundred. What for? He never stops looking and finding and looking and not finding and looking further on, further and further on, he never stops poking, reading, diving, going back up top. I never stop re-reading naturally I never re-read the same thing twice, and I have so far never managed to read, or rather to have read, I don't know how to read any other way than by coming back, I haunt, I come back to re-read I go back to re-read the same book differently, the more I read the more it stretches out, stands up, spreads out, shows up, on each re-reading I also turn up thousands of inner workings and traces besides the thousands and hundreds of thousands before, a book is as a hundred books for me over a few years. It takes up all my time. I always read the same two thousand books, assembled by the time I was 19, I had already re-read them several times when the-Book-that-I-never-read came along. Every year I re-read a few of the thousand that I know by heart without knowing them at all, as I know without knowing it Strasbourg Cathedral. Still unread. Each time I re-read a book it sets off a chain reaction. The brand new experience of re-reading an often re-read book causes changes throughout my difference engine. Having discovered tiny highly precise cogs that had thus far escaped me spurs me on to re-read a few other books differently. The most inexplicable thing is that the prophetic spirit spread throughout the whole geometric volume of my library. I do not choose my friends, I am chosen. The reason why, after years without a word, those I was quite distant from become, from one day to the next, closest of all, the most alive, the most thrilling, the vital ones, is never revealed to me. I am summoned. Three summers ago I was called by Melville – it works like an imperious telephone call, it never occurs to me to resist, it presents itself not as a desire but as an emergency. I was reading *Moby Dick*, when I had to read *Pierre* . . ., then *Under the Volcano*; just as there are gaps between each time and between the languages, each time is a different dream now in English, now in French or German, and everything is different. The day when I catch myself reading *The Shadow Line*, which I have never thought of re-reading since 1959, I realize all of a sudden that since 2005 I have been living off shipwrecks and trials, escorted by sperm whales and giants, for the last three years I have been living from one sea to the next, flanked by restless mountains, held fast by ice floes, at nighttime all is exile, mourning, amputation, prison hospitals, and that I am a visitor from beyond the grave amongst books that I have (re)read in the roaring 60s, those years when I mistook books for reality and there was no reality. In 2004 I was already making preparations for the expedition of the *Endurance* and I didn't know it. I see that Ernest Shackleton, the incredible storekeeper, regularly sets about making lists of supplies that will make it possible to *survive for six months* at the last extremity with no margin for error. He must only take across the most infernal Hells what he needs and not a single packet more, the extremely heavy loads must be intelligent and as light as possible.

30 boxes of matches;
6 and a half gallons of paraffin;
1 tin methylated spirit;
10 boxes of flamers;
1 box of blue lights;
2 Primus stoves with spare parts and prickers;
1 Nansen aluminium cooker;
6 sleeping bags;
A few spare socks;
A few candles and some blubber oil in an oil-bag.

Food:
3 cases sledging rations = 300 rations;
2 cases nut food = 200 rations;
2 cases biscuits: 600 biscuits;

1 case lump sugar;
30 packets of Trumilk;
1 tin of Bovril cubes;
1 tin of Cerebos salt;
36 gallons of water.

Instruments:
Sextant and charts
Binoculars
Prismatic compass
Aneroid barometer
Sea-anchor

You have to have *anticipated* through your imagination all the most unpredictable catastrophes: anticipate the unanticipatable. That can't be done in reality. It can be done in magic. Invisible and even inaudible voices guide us. Give a systematic description of what awaits us. Enumerate the three hundred and forty-two ropes in the rigging. In all cases the numbers are highly enigmatic. It's as if they were the names of hidden gods, and perhaps they themselves are the All-Powerful ones: 2711, 342, 600 + 8 + 5. They are bare. Clear. Round. Inflexible. Safe. Immovable. There are recipes, tricks, a whole technology of magic. You can see it in all the infernal explorations' expedition reports. Without the golden bough Aeneas would never make it as far as the underworld. The golden bough has such precision to it that it will be taken up later in the utmost detail by Babbage for the construction of his steel boughs. All the plans for machines designed for stays in the Last Extremity are not unrelated to the Golden Bough plan.

The number of fringes on the tallith, cited by J.D. in *Veils*: 600 + 8 + 5 knots. Number of food supplies, cited by

Sir Ernest Shackleton: 200 + 100 rations nut food + a case of biscuits (200) (Sledging rations) + one case of lump sugar + 28 packets of milk + 33 gallons of water + one tin of Bovril cubes + one tin of Cerebos salt. The number of golden leaves on the first bough: 150; with the bough torn away, another, also gold, grows back, and this branch comes to be covered in 200 leaves of the same metal. No one is granted access to the mysteries (you must twice cross the river that flows between life and death) unless he has removed and counted exactly the number of leaves then cut off the growth of golden hair whose numeric value is 13.

Around my head, in my bedroom and in my library, all these successive books generate a harsh climate, daubed with giant clouds announcing storms, I have floods everywhere, even in planes, trains, in museums, the ceilings of the dreams are swollen with heavy sheets of water.

The minute I got here with my mother, I *realized* that I immediately had to re-read *Wuthering Heights*, my son the astrophysicist had not yet left. The volume was not on my bookshelves. I bought the story again in a new edition last year, I have not re-read it and it wasn't there anymore. As soon as my son brought me a new copy from the city, a new, swarthy, coarse little volume, one of those paperbacks that absolutely *forbid* reading, the lost book re-appeared in the spot where my son and I had been looking for it. So everything had already started. I can't remember the details of the tragedy that day, I remember that everything is double, that there are so few names on the heights that everyone takes and so takes away the same names. The ill-effect of this is that everyone violently inhabits everyone. That morning, my son was still in the house, which is, incidentally, the one where he was born and which is the same age as him, all the trees have grown up with him, when a tall pine is torn up by a storm I cannot but feel targeted, the tree is like my son, I lose a tree I lose a son. But I had not yet discovered the Box.

From the insistence with which I go about demanding *Wuthering Heights* immediately, I have to have a copy of *Wuthering Heights this instant*, I have just arrived, three pines have been taken down by the January storm, and I want first of all and without delay a book that is not on my shelves, I have a sense that there are in those howling Heights of *Wuthering Heights* secret threads that I will be needing. I daren't tell my son that I am responding to a premonition. I lie. I say that I have to write an article on the narrative techniques. I could have told my son the truth, he is the best and the most astral being in the world, so nothing scares his science. It is my own mockery that I'm afraid of. There is no book that I can remember so poorly and so powerfully at the same time. Of the text, the sentences, all the powers of language . . . nothing. But my soul often gets lost in it: I remember having lived in flames beneath its vaults, I have the ground covered with ash and the pitiless sensation that all is lost, that there remains there the particular chill that takes hold when someone has paid insane homage to our name, has revered an unnameable being, worshipped a nightmare, in which you were yourself a terrible and terrified animal. I let out screams of rage into these same squally heights, this dream is incubating under the stairs, behind the windows, I did indeed know the character who was fearlessly malign, of hallowed blackness. Even now I know of people who see in him, a Heathcliff, only the most cultivated, the most faithful, the most loyal, the most touching of husbands. Even I, despite wishing I had never met him, cannot help but acknowledge *apart from myself* that had I not had the experience of the demon, something decisive in my story could not have taken place, and I would as a result not have had the good fortune of grace. But I was not thinking of this Emanation – I was rather expecting to find a knot in the rug of the text.

'Before we decide to read we try to keep chatting, to make a phone call,' said my friend Henry the other day. I am trying to decide to read, or to not decide to read, I thought. When I opened the Box, something was detonated: *you shall read*. It was all already decided. I underwent such a shock of admiration before destiny. How can I not start reading straight away? Start seeing, seeing the light of (a) day, never lived, coming back to have myself be seen

'It's either the book or the telephone,' he had said to me. 'You always see me with book because when I am at yours there is no phone. As soon as I get there I cut my phones off.' For me, it's a wonderful moment before he arrives, cutting my telephones off. Every time I head off to write, the first thing I do is cut off the phones. When the phone cuts off the thread of my thoughts, the pain I experience is not only caused by the blade, it's like scissors taken to my throat, the dreadful chopping sensation, the irruption of the assassin into the meadow of my texts, a going in for the kill. And the imposture of all those people who dial the wrong number and break into wherever I am, no, I say, that's not me, there's been a mistake, there's always a mistake. Nothing is more painful to me than the moment when the phone strikes. Carnage. The little corpses of thoughts, tiny, sliced up by the murderous knell of the ringing telephone, the bodiless heads of sentences cause me immense pangs of grief, I mourn these beings that I shall never know, I shed tiny tight-packed evaporated tears, a funeral cortège across my page. All that I wasn't able to write, will never write, strangled little spectres

88

– what was it you were you going to tell me? Sadly, I cannot draw speech from the dead.

My mother doesn't use the telephone anymore. She lives in a world where voices grope their way under the floorboards waters make masked, furtive apparitions on the threshold to her room, my house is a puppet show she says, it's Ssilly how the sentences squirm and only talk nonsense. Instead of telephony or phony, what's left is the last resort of navigation by paper: you sit yourself down in the skiff of a deck-top chair, and you weigh anchor out onto the Ocean. Various Oceans roll at will. 'Where are you?' I say. 'Off the coast of Tierra del Fuego?' 'Three different reds,' she says. My mother has a cane for a rudder. A bit of flotsam, but it does float.

Now I remember: in 1964, instead of living, I was on the phone, it's hard to imagine, I wonder myself how it is humanly possible to live by the cord, I didn't read *I was on the phone*, I didn't move because I was on the phone, whose mastercord was a three-meter long cord with its roots planted in my study, eat I would not, my grandmother would slide a porringer along the floor from which I only took so as the ghostly diving bell that I was could keep listening. Sometimes the telephone would talk for a while, a long while, talked for hours, kept talking. Sometimes the telephone withdrew into cowed silence, brooded, three years would go by, I turned to dust

I am writing this in the little room that I use as a study, my library and theatre, in which there is not the slightest trace of the wreck of the Telephone that happened in this very spot in 1965. I am almost offended at the idea that such a tragic and totally cruel and grotesque comedy could have taken place in this modest, monastic and remarkably sturdy study, from which dozens of my texts' expeditions have set off. Along the length of my arm one of my cats stretches out, gradually covers the table, extends her lilting warmth over the chapters: *The Human Condition: the last extremi-telephone* that I've put on the yellow folder; over the chapter *Forgetting of the names of Wuthering Heights*; and over the chapter: *Dad – very beautiful*. When Aletheia reaches a length of two metres, I will have to give in, stop writing. She shrinks back all of a sudden, turns over. Tricolour. Threecolours, says my mother.

Let's imagine that there had been time to install the telephone between Wuthering Heights and Thrushcross Grange. Would the dark and banished hero, whose name furrows and dominates the whole narrative with his asperities, have immediately ripped out the wires? Or would he, locked away in despair, have done his utmost to establish communication with the being on the other side that is him or that he is, who is him as her, she who is the soul outside of him, because of whom he is always casting himself out of himself in an attempt to take hold of himself once again? He hears her calling to him, it is his voice, he hears his 'name' ringing out across the woods, the moors, *Heathcliff* runs clothed in Her voice – it is not a name, it's a piece of God, it's a cliff-face that tips and a forest that walks. Marked on the backs of the chairs, on the bedsteads and on the lintels of the chimneybreasts, on the wood of the prayer stools and on the bedroom's burnt-out lime, the initials HC repeated as a lamentation, it is as if they were roaring like the wind and no one knows who is roaring, whether it be Heathcliff or Her, for the letters change shape with each signing. He is a real wanderer, I imagine a tormented ghost, not a haunter drawn to a place, anchored to a rampart, but a sort of fiery fool, a fear-stricken Orpheus, someone who hunts all over knowing very well that there is nowhere and no one. Henry also signs his passage, but it is without rage and without the hatred of despair that spurs Heathcliff. He paints our lives on the walls and on the wood of the bookshelves, in brief messages, a date two lines six words, and in the end the room looks like Montaigne's heavens – the starry and the sententious. But all that is painted and caressed, and not gouged out by claws.

I do not want to understand the propensity for madness that this writing chest contains. There is a secret there. What does it matter if in the end I die without having taken control of it, as long as it is always there, a free captive, and ageless. This secret has powers that have never weakened. The secret's secret is that it draws its powers from *someone*. This is where my meditation comes to a halt for as soon as I seem to begin asking myself who holds the keys to the secret, a throng rushes in as the pack of shades hurries to talk to Ulysses, me first, me first. What pains me is seeing the jumble of pathetic beggars – people who until the end did not know one another, some of them dear, some adored, some insignificant, some hated – and that the dream groups together, mixes up, undifferentiates without care without tact, on the pretence of reminding us that before the Truth of the Last Extremity all the individuals whom we have come across in our time have left an equal mark on the wall. Who knows, then, which hero, which hapless dolt, which leaseholder, might be the pretender to the keys.

The air in my library is subject to savage variations. From hurricane to sleep. As is the case in all real Libraries, angel-devil boxes that they are.

I go in – the cube is small, which accentuates the violence of these rages, its sixteen square metres are always full. In the container, reveries take hold in a minute – and in the moment when I slip down to my table, I am in hypnogogia: in this climate that precedes my falling – not sleep, hypnosis – the walls fall away between times. I write on a fall of walls covered with ancient graffiti. How many passers-by have left their signatures here. No sleep but a halfwakefulness that travels a few narrow centuries *every minute*. Land and languages are twinned. Or else I am unknowingly in a hypnopompic state. I go. I recognize the wild expanse of moorland, sojourn of faeries, the inconsolable, the restless, the beyond-time's-pale. If what was declared by the name Prénom de Dieu were scored into some wall or trunk the mental elasticity of my library could have borne it. The unforeseen element in this story is this bookcase – a sort of cardboard still painted white – which will have been so in the end. I have come to confer upon this place the attributes of the sacred. I convince myself that as soon as I enter, the voices of writing close in and that if I sought to go to work elsewhere they would not address me. I'll do everything in my power I say to myself never to be banished from this sanctuary. I see threats approaching, but I cast them off. If we have to transport my mother who is part of the sanctuary by ambulance we'll do it. I do not know how we shall end. I do not know how we arrived at this point of pine and twine.

And here, in this place that has become for me another self, there has as far as I know never been a copy of that book. The stock is in the Box.

♪

As soon as I closed the Box – whereas my heart was wide open, my blood sprang with Joy, I laughed, I laughed – and packed it up, pushed it away, shut it back up in its box of oblivion, I thought that never again could I not read these objects, especially the manuscripts, because I am conscious and awake in 2009. There are no longer things that I do under hypnosis, except dreams. But 'logically', I thought, I first have to read *the book*, I thought. This 'logically' calls for commentary: I owe myself to *the book*, I thought. That's what I'm thinking. I have to go from the book to the manuscript, and not from the manuscript to the book. This obvious fact seemed to me irrefutable. A week hence I will think it arbitrary, but steps had already been taken. After all, it is *the book* that I have always been afraid of. Even the *absolute* authority of J. D. over my opinions and judgments could not bring me to read it. That gives a sense of the fear, that strange, tough, indecipherable animal and whose name moans *feeaaeeaar*. Fear has no why. That is why it reigns. No one knows who or what to attack. I would really like to know how to tell the truth, but I only have to claim to tell one for it to be false. Tell, no. The facts: (1) I have cut myself loose from absolute authority, like the first man. It's stupid and it's something we do. Not that J. D. had ordered me to read, since he did not know that I had not read the book he was talking to me about, such that I should have felt obliged for all manner of reasons (curiosity, honesty, politeness) to acquaint myself with the object. I had thus been able to disobey without disobeying. I had slid beneath the cloak of a silence. I was lying and I drowned the lie in a foggy mien. He never found out that this book of which he ardently spoke to me, and perhaps all the more keenly for the fact that he believed that naturally I had read it, was entirely unknown to me. Telling him that I knew nothing of it would have led to giving explanations. He would not have believed me. He would have believed me. I could not have masked my malady. I could not have borne his disapproval. His astonishment. His indulgence. His compassion. His religious horror. What is a book whose father, author, creator, manu-facturer, -fabricator, -motor, inventor knows nothing

93

about it? What is a book, then? And you? And me? *Who* wrote it? That is the question! Someone? Someone did it, someone screamed, someone signed, but who? We shall *never* get as far as this interrogation, I say to myself, I am too afraid. In 1997 when he spoke to me with warmth and a great deal of admiration of childlike purity, when I rediscovered the importance that he had discovered he reminded me in 1965, I did all I could to protect myself, I huddled down against the storm, no one had yet read such a book in 1965, he said. 'Nor had Henry, in truth, back in 1965 he had the mindset of Ernest Shackleton,' he said, 'You know who I mean?' 'Yes, I know Ernest Shackleton,' I said, 'a pure genius,' I said and without affectation, without affectation, who undaringly dares to embark upon the deciphering of nameless regions of the Antarctic Continent, the Freud of the ice, with his only reward and pride that of having been the first not to quake before such a world, a world as other as the world and in all things, a world of colossi in all whites (blues, golds, because whites are all in colours that do not exist, except in Antarctica, even in paintings painters have not dreamt of them). Even in photographs I cannot contemplate these forms of beauty that are so other, excessive, wild, round and that all signify: 'nothings that you are, we are man's unbelievables', without being seized by an annihilation anxiety, for there is nothing on this continent that consents or relates to man. But we were getting lost in these majesties animated by Titanesque moods, and where only the whales knew happiness. He was drifting. He wanted to talk about this unnatural book. And I was doing all I could so that the breath was bellowed far above my head. I can see myself mentally curled up like a hedgehog, afraid that at any moment a word, an image, might touch me, cowering in a dug-out, waiting for It to pass.

One day in 1994, on the telephone, J. D. said to me: 'I've just re-read (the Thing). There's everything in there.' That 'everything' had both frightened and saved me. After all, 'everything' is nothing. I branched off. I started talking about Rousseau. I diverted him, I set him drifting off towards other lines drawn around the last lake, the lake of the Last Extremity, lake of farewells to the world before the confinement to St Peter's Island, or the isle of la Motte for the rest of his days. It's a lake in the shape of an O. A miracle lake that makes Os spring up all over. All the pages are a path scattered with Os, in all colours, in all sorrows, of all schemes, all prayers, until the prayer of the last extremity, you remember, I say, the one that Rousseau got from the old woman whose whole prayer was an O. 'I have ever been passionately fond of water,' he says, J. D. saying the innocent sentence that he took from Rousseau.

Another time, it was in 1999, he tells me: 'There's even the tallith with fringes' and ever since I have not been able to forget the thing. It is the only 'thing' that I know. Apart from the shawl and the fringes that came out, I threw myself into guarding the sepulture with the secret inside.

He was congratulating himself by now for having been the first. And so the only. He is always still the first and the only, I thought. The first is always also the last, I thought. There will be no more Shackleton. The first men to have walked on the moon, that's nothing. In 1969, forty years ago exactly, I watched them with my children, and even then I thought 'What about Shackleton?' They walk on Shackleton's moon fifty years after him they spend twenty-two hours revived every second by millions of cameras. But the first and last will have existed in sur-existence for twenty-four months without a Witness, the Styx and the Acheron crossed twenty-four times between 1914 and 1916.

As for the book that J. D. was talking about, it filled me with horror. A Fear tall as an ice cliff – the unbearable thought that this book was 'great' as J.D. – in whom I have always had confidence – put it. If that was the case I could not be its 'author'. I bitterly regretted it. Or else it was, it was infinitely greater than me, I couldn't conceive of it. Then I must have been the Author's medium. I was humiliated, frightened, tiny, nameless. Not only was I dispossessed, but I should also accuse myself of imposture. I would only have signed someone else's work. Who knows, perhaps I was just a sort of stand-in bearing the name of a god, and what a name! At least the name was primitive. HC. I'll come back to this. Every compliment, bit of praise, flattery, falls upon me as if I had just committed a fraud – for it was not me who wrote those texts, I am not the person who wrote them. I can't even say that at one time I was. The total effacement of the origin authorizes all hypotheses.

I will have had courage enough to examine the object.

What stopped me was SurFear. I was afraid of having an image of the author on her sickbed – I hate lunatics and amnesiacs. But beyond that fear I surfeared perhaps meeting a force stronger than mine, with which I could not compete, that wasn't me, and which I could only have known in a dream and in another life.

No one has ever read this book. Henry came to me through *Inside*. And this book has been out of print for so many years that I had ended up thinking that it would waste away, like those children whom you don't hear anything about anymore except that they are dead, those children who were only ever dead and whose name is the only thing to live, live on, survive, as if a dead child were only born to be the bearer of a name, whose power has to be preserved at the cost of human sacrifices. That is how a son had died for Heathcliff without leaving any real trace, even a ghostly one. He was merely dead. A half-line. Take away his first name and use it to make up all the names for the Stranger. What is a son? He can be left for dead, son of the dead. Authors die of the dead son.

I wonder which son's name was taken away to make the proper name of the Prénom de Dieu.

§

Even when I systematically examined the entirety of the Box, I never *read* the stories. Except the titles. There is disorder and yet all is calm inside the Box. It lets me do as I wish, like a seal when it has never yet seen a human. Enormous strength, defenceless. The typed copies came back, went off again, I could believe that it was some others, it was the same ones, but sometimes without a title sometimes with. All the titles are completely foreign to me. Some I had heard of, at some time or another, though I won't swear to it. What I *saw*: the texture of the writing, the shape is so not me, a full, fat, round figure arranges steadily, calmly, a sort of Little Red Riding hood, I say to myself, nothing like the craggy taught sinewy tense hasty lettering that I use now. I see that I am looking at it with curiosity, sympathy, like a mother at the nursery gates, full-cheeked, a spring in the step, sturdy, unaffected, and plucky, she reminds me of someone dauntless, nothing like mine and it's . . . Albertine. This has taken me by surprise. I quite like the fact that a delinquent has swung into my place. But it's just an appearance. I thought I saw a booming voice.

Today again. 16 July. Again not read. Already forgotten, immediately in that moment forgotten even the titles that

I've just seen. A *Wuthering Heights* effect has spread out in the depths: there is still the wailing, the eternal pain of a black boy. Seen a little: all over the pages the word *son*. Principally. The word, son of God I tell myself. The word son is a son

THE LAKE

But it's not the word son that has struck me. Here is where I am putting the Striking Discovery:

Circumstances: it happened at five o'clock in the morning and I had just 'read' in Proust's notebooks

which Henry had given me as a present the day when I cried in the little room of manuscripts that my fore-keeper was showing me, firstly at the sight of Saint-Simon's row of tears; secondly at the sight of the unforgettable smudge of Pascal's tears of joy, thinking that tears well up at the sight of traces of tears on paper, because we feel sadness more acutely in things that have been wept for us onto paper fibres, I said to myself; and thirdly at the sight of some pages from the end of *Time Regained* where there is nothing left but the Last Extremity, which is reached by its own limit, the paper goes no further than the edge, and yet the abyss still must be saturated, and since there are no more than a few centimetres of space and a few breaths of time, then it's writing that has to *evolve*, like any endangered species it has to mutate or die, and it can't want to be able to die, so it mutates, it becomes the size of a bacterium, it shrinks, tinifies itself, turns into no more than mites and micromites, oh how this nanographic metamorphosis must aggrieve the dying signatory, it is a gigantic germ war against the Forces of Finality. In the end I could no longer see its germy feet, bane of my life, power of superhuman miniaturization of a soul that will not give up, and, with this, tears diluted the all but invisible object, and I did not even see it disappear

the fragment for love of which Henry had given me this vital volume in 2005, on 13 February with the epigraph: *another-ranniversary*, in reference to the date when we commemorate my father's death and resurrection

I have never stopped re-reading that fragment. It has always delighted me by the oddness of its construction, its magical wording, the painter's pure cheek of impetu and abbrev the passing of a ray of light cast by a half-setting sun on a philosophical vision. (I am writing this in the hours that follow the Striking Discovery.)

Here is the fragment:
'Mettre à Balbec et à Venise une femme faisant de l'aquarelle (regarder l'aq. Brouardel la falaise lointaine et de Doncières (non autre nom) et le clocher de la Salute (pas Salute regarder l'aq.)'
['Put a woman doing aquarelle in Balbec and Venice (look at Brouardel w. for distant cliff ~~and~~ de Doncières (not other name) and the bell-tower of la Salute (not Salute look at w.)']

ε

Ever since that 13 February 2005, which has taken on the
bronze sheen of a day's reading long, long ago, so profound
was the effect of that extraordinarily whimsical sort-of sentence, this fragment has powers over me comparable to the
title *François le Champi* over the narrator of *Time Regained*,
every time I think of it and every time it comes back into my
mind, and every time, having mislaid it, I go looking for it,
find it, copy it out by hand once again, as if passing my hand
over its surface with such complex features were going to help
me to draw verses from its nose, on the one hand there rises in
me the young woman of letters, the one who I am today with
Henry, who is also still of letters but differently than me, just
as ever since the first day – and it's that young woman barely
born into the kingdom who takes up her place in my place
in me – in these times of the Box –, she who has received the
sentence like a new, strangely wrought ring, the magic ring,
the mythical ring, an invention, efficacious, great lovers of
sentences with secrets: we imagine ourselves gently rubbing
the ring, until as if summoned by a telephone call, someone,
probably the genie of the sentence, sends answers to the thousand questions that we should like to ask. And on the other
hand, today it's 'the person from another time' who I am, so
close to the dead and so keen, tireless and yet impatient and
troubled who stalks, circles, persecutes this fragment. I end
up calling it the Fragment, then the Frag Ment. The word,
instead of easing off, steps up, comes closer to a key word like
Heathcliff, grows strange and takes on the status of an enigmatic title. I say *Frag ment* and I hear in German, in English,
in languages, that there is a number in there. No doubt about
it, for William Legrand's disciple that *Frag ment* could well be:
the question (or the questioner) meant.

101

I cannot shake this Frag ment. I read it as I read it once and as I shan't finish reading it, on the one hand with the same melancholy effect that I felt on 13 February 2005, a melancholy tinged with a burst of joy, on seeing with my own eyes how literary tears never dry, with, on the other hand, the same certainty that there is in the Text a treasure that I want to possess and which is, so I believe, the recipe for the immortality of things, that I do not know how to obtain it, deserve it, earn it, conquer it perhaps, but that at least I may, by chance, locate.

This fragment is my book of spells. This Frag ment is Proof. I station myself before its doorway faithful as a hound. I am its hound. I lick its feet, its hands, its words, its mysteries. *'Put a woman doing aquarelle in Balbec and Venice.'* A painterly sentence! And the painter is in the poet. I must paint a woman painting, they say to themselves, I shall paint myself painting a woman painting, already I can see myself painting this woman, and the secret of this painting is the *aquarelle* the essence of the thing is that this woman is painting with water, in this there is, unseen but felt, a deposit of tears. Aquarelle woman in B. and V.

And that *Mettre!* that Put! I say to myself. Isn't the whole force of Fragment in this: *Mettre! Mettre* I say to myself is the encrypted *maître*, the encrypted master, of this great project. *Mettre* can only be *Maître* in French. I hear the poet using this imperative infinitive, the one within the other, order and advice, authority, intimation. And all is magnified: *Mettre*, in Balbec and in Venice, a woman, tie a woman to the necks of these divinities, to the collars of these magnificently named felines. Balbec in the background and to the right, Venice in the foreground and to the left or Balbec back left, all combinations are open. If we add to this the fact that Balbec

102

is a fictional place and Venice a real place, or vice versa, that one is just as fictional, the other is as real as the other, we've got the abc of fiction, my daughter says. Real fiction. Verifiction, Henry says. I gave you the *Recipe*, Henry told me. The Recipe of Recipes: you *put words side by side sticking* faithfully to the mysterious instructions (keep in the oddities of punctuation, the indentations, the ellipses, the abbreviations) and it makes a THING. A literary object. The work of a *Maître*. Not forgetting the *l'aq*. the formula for tears. Note that each word side by side with the word of the other side is the first name of a world, its abc. Its Egyptian bug. If there is a kaleidoscope that brings together all the coloured scales fallen from the eyes of Proust like broken stained glass from a cathedral, it is this object. If there is a gold-bug the size of a nut with two jet stains on the back at one end and a third, a little more elongated, in black lacquer at the other and with antennae *invisibly drawn* in, it is this object. I felt as if I had just met William Legrand. As if William Legrand, whom I had previously thought deranged, that is, William Proust, taking the time for a pedagogical demonstration, with the generosity that intellectual triumph arouses in a mind that has suffered, was in the process of conveying to me the *Secret of Secrets*, the Gold Secret hidden within all secrets of all kinds. And what is astounding is that the Secret of Secrets is written out *letter by letter* hidden in invisible ink on a sheet where it is all at once dissolved, having been written, blacked out such that one can quite easily see nothing at all, and not think for a moment that there is a secret there somewhere since by definition the secret has been carried off, worn down, wiped out, disappeared, faded away, and that, however deleted, gagged, foreclosed it is, by the most mysterious, but not explicable, paths of revelation, it comes irresistibly to *penetrate* some unforeseen addressee who admits its *presentiment*. For all this takes place in the other-reality the length of

103

which William Proust just as Legrand will obstinately have paced.

We will have long since found out that the Secret of Secrets is a matter of *reading* signs. All secrets are written. They live in the dispersal of a language whose elements are for the most part confused with the elements found in Nature, as a Body ripe for Resurrection. All secrets can hibernate for human generations.

To be the receiver of a secret, says William Legrand – that is, Proust –, you just need to have the pure luck not to miss the many signs cast into the beneficiary's path: (1) the Secret is only revived following an *extraordinary series* of accidents and coincidences. (2) And so you have to be blessed with sensitivity and an indefatigable constancy. You have to be capable of believing even the absurd and simultaneously have the temperament of a logician and brilliant sage – to seize the moment of illumination, archimedically. With the number of conditions and circumstances being very high, we must lend a flame to this kindling, add the spark that lights an improbable fire in a hearth, because it is never cold enough for a fire, except one day every five or ten years. Yet and so all the events that determine access to the secret (from contact with the linen, noise common both to a *spoon* touching a plate and to a hammer striking a wheel, and from the woman doing aquarelle in Balbec or Venice, from the steps on the paving stones of the Guermantes courtyard and the courtyard of the Hôtel Richelieu, down to the number of capital letters, or proper names, abnormally high, along with the number of imperatives in the fragment's wording) of the gold-bug's piece of vellum *happen on this one* day. Without this cold, no fire. Without this fire, no heat able perhaps to bring the dead vellum back to life. Without the dog jumping up at the host seated not far from the fire, no nearing of the dead vellum to the reach of the heat, and afterwards without the projection of the gold-bug by Jupiter first by the bad eye, first moment of the failed experiment, then, by the good eye, discovery of the Treasure, at the last extremity, no resurrection of the Balbec dining room with its damasked linen laid out like altar cloths to receive the gold of the sunset so as to shake from within the stability of the Hôtel de Guermantes, to force its doors, open the place up to an invasion by Venice, which is to say Balbec, no propagation of fleeting fragment of eternity, by the texts' telepathic wires.

I am convinced that *The Gold-Bug* is Proust's secret talisman, I said, he doesn't quote it anywhere, said Henry, that's the proof, the proof of the Secret, the narrator has only left the most imperceptible and in any case fruitless of traces, he grants Poe the space of a mere three letters of his surname, or two millimetres, in a company of madmen discredited by his grandmother, composed of one Baudelaire one Verlaine one Rimbaud and one Poe, half of a poet, and out of obedience to love, to the behest of grandmother's happiness, to her certainty that in the interests of the species this son would do well to counterpoise his nervous disposition by frequenting persons of tact, refinement and discretion, he will have done his utmost to expunge all trace of his frequenting those creatures that choose suffering over appeasement, he cannot not have read *The Gold-Bug* and, as soon as his colossal fortune was made, buried it beneath the roots of the giant Tulip tree *liriodendron tulipiferum* – the tallest and the most Proustian of literature trees that ever stood on the coast of South Carolina. Without my visit to the manuscripts department of the Bibliothèque Nationale de France no tears, without the story about tears for Henry no well-meaning consolation in the form of a book, without the mysterious intuition that leads him to countersign the three-line quotation that at first sight was of no exceptional interest, without the presentiment that ties me blindly to my paper-bug, without the large and precise number of circumstances, which I have yet to count, no Resurrection.

Let's suppose that the first Circumstance essential to the Striking Discovery will have been the re-reading of the Bug Fragment. I linger over this. Until the sun comes back up. Which is when

Just then, on 1 July, as if in a dream there was a thunder-clap that no one hears except me. Bangbababang! Again. Bangbangbang! Someone is trying to stop me. A tornado grabs the garden by the hair shakes it in all directions pelts it with blows turns it on its own axis and kills it. In a matter of seconds. What is stronger than love and stronger than death is Resistance

Just then –

I don't know at what moment exactly, the moment M, I receive the revelation of a word. Revelation is the word. A flash. The word has to be short. Crash! There is something more than *crash*! A rip in the night. I saw it: smash! We see, we hurry. The night keeps mum. In another time. It's that key-moment that I want to get to, I should have done it a few days ago, I prepared myself for it from 2 July, I couldn't do it, it wasn't possible before then, I thought that I would forget, that it would disappear, like the others, but it remains. Manuscript. All strength is in the hand.

At a certain moment then, I saw, *I saw* in the corner diago-nally opposite the one where William Legrand will have seen the image of a *Kid*, a young goat, in three letters in his language, a three-letter word, like *a kind of signature*, and which was where the title of one of the stories should have been. A heading. *Le Lac* [The Lake]. I say 'a kind of signature', whereas *Le Lac* is inserted on the top left of the body of the document, as any title would be, but the script was such that it had the appearance of a seal.

I have always written with my hands, steeped, rummaged, rubbed, sifted, hands in the viscera and blood of dreams, and hands in the pungent sludge of the passions, I have written by touch, I have always felt my way, I walk barefoot across the paper, I look at the bodies with my fingers. I write joined up, I knot one letter to another, I lace, I fasten.

But *that Lac* is not by my hand. It is delicate, fine, pared down, musical, each letter, perched on its stave, the l, the a, the c, separated by an interval, and with a single line gap in between, such that it has the appearance of musical notation

&

And yet I was the one who had had the key since 13 February 2005, and there was no door.

I was in front of this fragment, enchanted and enchanted at being mystified. What an *incomprehensible* and movable pleasure. Now I delight in the decision to put a woman-doing-aquarelle, in Balbec and in Venice, either at the same time in the two cities, or at intervals (or in the idea of somewhere in a text putting a woman-doing-aquarelle-in-Balbec-and-in-Venice as in the painting of a Pre-Raphaelite painter's dream), now I spend hours re-playing the notes of the parenthesis (no other name) no, other name's name, no-other name, savouring the alliteration's song, the name of the

107

same name as the other, now it's the cliff that is a cliff and is not a cliff is a bell-tower that isn't a bell-tower

And each time the ringing of the autograph: *look at the* l'aq.*! look at the* l'aq.*!*

If you manage to *look at the* l'aq., you are joyously uplifted by the certainty of succeeding in seeing the secret. It suddenly occurs to me that perhaps 'the woman' is not doing *l'aquarelle* of Balbec and Venice at all, that she is perhaps not doing *l'aquarelle* of Balbec in Venice or of Venice in Balbec. Perhaps she is *doing l'aquarelle* of an interior garden. Until I have looked at and seen the *l'aq.* I shan't know

20 July

You cannot imagine the number of Hitches, Hold-ups, Interruptions that accompany the Story on its pilgrimage. As soon as it is on the right path, obstacles spring up beneath the feet of the pages. There would be no secret without this tyranny that protects it, forbids it and engenders all around a climate of devastation and sacrifice. As you approach the famous Tulip Tree it is as if the night were at the wrong moment pouncing on the breaking day and closing its jaws around its head.

L e L a c in pencil. The very lovely interval of a major third. You can hear the voice gently rising. La, fa!

At this point I notice the pencil's *endurance*. Its stroke has kept a freshness that no ink could have preserved. Perhaps it is this untouched youth that touches me at first. Between the Pencil and the Box, a certain harmony – a magical way of dispensing with time. Of remaining spared.

Whereas the pages of my handwriting are embalmed, the strong round form gripped and faded by ages.

In amongst these hundreds of sheets either typed out in multiple copies or written out by hand by this or that HC, she or he who no longer lived in me but was still at large in the texts of these 'stories', in amongst these strangers – for this whole period was populated, I saw as much at first glance, by a multitude of people whom I recognized not at all, and who were surrounding him, by many strange and foreign names *one could see only him.* As William Legrand only saw the little gold-bug in amongst a tropical flora and fauna, which is to say exactly as the Prince de Guermantes only appeared to the narrator *comme si doré*, as if golden, like the charming prince in amongst real beings with a golden soul enclosed in his name which is also his person, which is to say as the musical notes *si do re*, as the narrator implies. As *si do re*, as no one, as impalpable, *Le L/a/c*, like an apparition of a musical magic lantern. Or even, it is as if in a dream I had just discovered the apples of the Hesperides, or rather the Desperides. I am quite aware that there is gold in the air, and that gold is something other than gold in the interior world. My lantern was lit, in a single stroke of the pencil. *'Look at the* l'aq.*!'*

All this is of course merely the most extraordinary of coincidences.

There is nothing more 'treasure' than this pencilled *Lac*, and many times treasure. (1) I was not looking for it. (2) This *Lac is in J. D.'s handwriting.* (3) It could, as a title and as a word, easily have been erased with a stroke of the rubber. (4) As soon as I set eyes on it I am dazzled by the ciphered link between the *l'aq.* from my Fragment in the French and this title traced in pencil. (5) And yet thinking about it later, I shall be led to doubt that there is any link other than by pure accident. This fills me with wonder beyond all wonderment. Let us not forget that nor is there any link whatsoever between the gold-bug, which looks like gold and isn't, and the treasure discovered by William Legrand *on the pretext* of the gold-bug. And what is most extraordinary is that up until the last extremity I thought that in the end the treasure would elude, like all treasure, our enlightened hero's spade, that he would bring to light just an empty hole, the sole treasure having only ever been the little dead bug. Remains of an initiation. The bug's one necessity will only ever have been for show and trickery. I believed in the bug. I didn't believe in the treasure except as looted and vanished. And it's the treasure that's the true and unbelievable outcome of any reading of *The Gold-Bug*. In the end it would be a mistake to believe that the gold-bug was not possessed of occult powers. It serves no purpose. Without 'it', that is, without the phantasmagoria that it spawns in the characters' minds, never would our characters have striven to creep clamber and fall upon the treasure. It is by mistake that we reach the secret, that is, by faith, which is what makes the mistake and the way there. The Bug's power is all the greater because it is fictitious. Baudelaire is mad about Poe as the greatest philosophical trickster in all literature. And so there are two of them to the one madman – Poe, and Baudelaire, who is Poe in French. Poe died for Baudelaire. Baudelaire is the resurrection of Poe. Each is the other's bug. They each set the other to work on the treasure. The inventory of the treasure will always be beyond my imagination, but not the narrator's banking skills, who shows himself at last to be as good an accountant as he is expert a chemist. In an instant, the first, a treasure of incalculable value blooms, dazzling, before us. In this first instant the Subject surpasses the teller. The teller says he doesn't want to describe the feelings with which he contemplates the treasure. The teller says he supposes himself dumbfounded.

At the sight of the *L a c* I am myself in the supposition of this state. The beams from my lanterns send flashes and splendours flying up from the box that *positively* splash your eyes. Being unable to describe my feelings I borrow from the friends of William Legrand their apocalyptic material. Their teller tells the following feeble words: (Legrand is) *exhausted with excitement.* Jupiter *seems stupefied, thunderstricken.* He falls to his knees in the chest, plunges his bare arms into the gold up to the elbows, leaves them there for a long while, as if enjoying the voluptuous pleasures of a bath. All – William Legrand, Edgar Poe, Baudelaire – turn about this ocean of gold. Thus, with splashed eyes, I turn about the *L a c* and I plunge my naked eyes between the gold letters and leave them there a good while, as if I were at pains, so entranced was I, to find the wording of a look. Such a meagre word, such a profound story. It was nonetheless necessary for you to *awaken so to speak*, says Baudelaire gently lifting Edgar Poe out of his indescribable transport. One can be *as if* asleep, though awake. It is a case of *sleepwaking*.[7] And so it's very difficult to come to whilst awake since you never know which side of the ecstasy you are on. I often witness this ecstasy in my mother when she is mentally up to her elbows in geraniums. 'What day is it?' she murmurs. 'Monday,' I say. 'What day is Monday?' murmurs the bedazzled one. 'The first one,' I say. 'What month?' 'July.' 'Ah. And the children?' 'We'll see them in August. After July.' 'That's nice.' And all that from the fourcolours! It's very beautiful. The day. In this state we can see the secret connections between flowers children

---

[7] In English in the original.

colours the daily resurrection from death as a gateway to the next life. A revelation that Poe passes on to his heir on the day of his death. His. Death carries.

In a second moment, seven hours later, the teller, after setting the Subject's belongings amongst the brambles and under the guard of the Dog with strict orders from Jupiter not *to open its mouth* upon any pretence, and after examination of the treasure and careful re-ordering, at last surpasses the real Subject, the supposed Subject of all Suppositions. And everything was ordered and auric old ages ago. All the details are available in the text and the whole thing has been valued at one and a half million dollars and later at much more than that sum which constantly increases as reality exceeds fiction, once placed in order.

23 July

Put here, in the place where I can 'see' in my mind my mother and Jupiter in a gold bath, situated 'post-ordering' of two skeletons put on the grave to keep off intruders. When I am the double poet in a state of resurrection I am deep in fiction's most extra-real thicket to the point of *omitting* entirely the persistence of a Real Reality, which has no shortage of thrills of its own. But one morning when I find myself back there, it will come back to me, as reality R, a detail of the utmost oddity, in the form of an envelope from the house of *Bo. Funeral Directors*, which has since 1820 had charge of letters, that is, of the fate of letters in cases of burial. This letter concerns the remains. It is not this that strikes me. It is the return of implausibility within reality R itself. My grave, which is to say my mother's, has for some years lived next to Baudelaire's tomb. At first I had my reservations about such close quarters, a fantasmatic discomfiture at hurrying into the throng of Shades on the uncertain banks of the Acheron, side by side with Baudelaire, skull somewhat in disarray – as if in a dream. I find myself side by side in the same Nothingness bed, on 20 July, with the famous man of the theatre P. Chevreau. It takes me a few moments to make sense of this familiarity which from a certain point of view embarrasses me, whereas I cannot deny the authenticity and the simplicity of the connection: I am in the state of the narrator of the *Bug* to whom William Legrand reveals that he has a secret and at the same time quite illegitimate and undeniable connection with the spirit of the famous Chevreau, the infamous Pirate himself, the master and he who had been dispossessed of the Treasure of treasures, Kidd, the captain of the unconscious of all adventurers of the last extremities. 'Remember,' I said to my daughter, 'that William Legrand reminds Edgar Poe, who passes it on to Baudelaire, that he discovered in the corner of the parchment the traces of a figure depicting a *kid*, and not a goat.' The figure of this animal, Baudelaire tells me in our dream, must be considered a kind of logogriphic or hieroglyphic signature (Kid, young goat). 'At no point,' I say to my daughter, 'do I think to link these tombs, it doesn't even occur to me to re-read the tombs of Baudelaire and Poe, put side by side by Mallarmé. My memory lives in Oblivion,' I say to my daughter, 'I see it as a bewitchment produced by the Box.'

☩

I circle the *Lac*. It is a *literary object*, though at first you might think it's a reservoir of water, a hole but full, a pond but big, that it's a tank of monsters and melancholies, for reasons obscure, the lake has a force that overflows it. Why it attracts poems no one knows, that's what interests me, I trail the leman's tracks to lake, lake's shores are haunted by swooners and sweetings, there is no knowing whether Lamartine's name would have survived without his *Lake*, all the mysterious fortune of the name Lamartine is the result of an incantation with the hidden force of a lake, that is of the lake, of the enigmatic *lac*citude of the lake, of the empty repetition of the words oh lake oh lake that hypnotize those along the shore. Rousseau will have returned to the spirit of the lake the immortality he borrowed from it, all of his Passion runs on the water from his lake, on the tears of his many walkers, as everything takes place from one shore to the other, it is no use circling the lake since the other shore is always behind me the moment I think I've got there. Some go Lake's way, some the way of Ocean, depending on whether we're by the way of the ring or the way of the Spume. The lake is a vast sack of reveries. Whereas up on the Moors lies not reverie but madness.

My surprise is all the more acute for the fact that, when my gaze is brought up short at this word just as the tip of the narrator's boot stumbles on an iron ring which, lying half entombed beneath a mound of fresh earth, ensnares, en*lac*es, him, I am not lakelike.

£>

Nor is J. D. Besides, he will have been the first to confide that he was born a stranger to the 'lake' as a feature of the landscape that does not exist in the country of his birth. Born a stranger to expanses of water – the lack of that country's dry soil. And yet the word *lac*, which is to say the term as a shard of sound, lactic leftover of the mother's crest,[8] will have been

---

8 The French is *seing*, an archaic word for signature and a homophone of *sein* (breast).

his signature syllable, his pocket puddle, his object of secrets, in 1965 an as yet unidentified star but there it already *lay* – *c*oming to ripen in his sky.

I didn't know I was a lady of the lake, I say to myself – neither as a woman or man strolling through Literature nor as a woman strolling through reality. In reality the key is double and even more than double. I can't even try to analyse the incessant activity of the tribe of lakes. The stupefaction at seeing these words bearing J. D.'s handwriting dominates I think all other feelings. When I want to talk to my daughter about it the following day, I tell her a story that I try to make faithful to the inaugural scene. I am pleased to see her surprise no different from mine. 'I can see the title (of a text entirely plunged into the depths of oblivion). It's *Le Lac*. And it is not my handwriting,' I say. 'Ah,' cries my daughter, 'whose handwriting is it then?' 'J. D.'s,' I say. 'Well well!' says my daughter. 'So this story, he gave it a nickname, did he?' 'A nickname?' 'He gave it another name?' 'No, I say. It didn't have one. Neither first name nor last.'

Of that I was sure. In 1965 the larvae still appeared without extremities or heads, or titles, without name without signature without logogriph. 'He gave it its name,' I say. I also say something of the total ablation of all trace of this text in my head, which accounts for my forgetting its name. I'll try to describe my current state of anxiety: a desire, a hope, but so faint, of rediscovering the 'memory' twitching behind the title's curtain. I am in the almost painful state of the creature who hears the strains of a *quartet* by Vinteuil *through the door* (I can hear the first notes of a piece, in gold, through the door of the box) although he has long since *exhausted* the joys of listening to a Vinteuil sonata, such that he finds himself in the same mourning and the same despondency that had struck him as when, having *exhausted* the joys that lay in the hawthorn and wanting no more to ask as much of another flower than my mother of another flower than the geranium – so, when all is dried up, and, as must be underscored, since he does not wish to fight against this drying up, for its cause is his attachment to his first unforgettable but *exhausted* hawthorn –, there comes the *Moment of an I saw*: once long ago it was the appearance of a bush of pink thorns, spectre of the Hawthorn and promise of new joys, and now it is the sign of a resurrectional dawn, the first bars of the resurrection incarnated by the quartet, son of the sonata and the return of Joy, the same and yet not the same, the old and yet the new, the one and only and yet the next. Notes in pencil. Hesitation of a baptism. I start circling this use of lead. What are we doing when we write in pencil? When we pencil in a number with a preparation that leaves characters both perishable and yet as durable as if they were drawn in smalt? We let luck and chance into the game. Now there is a name that slips in unnoticed.

Here, it occurs to me that *Le Lac* is perhaps only, will have been only a spectre, an aborted larva, a supplicant whose entry into the world of people will no doubt have been refused. I grow sure of it: there is no one by that name in the book. This possibility is soon reinforced by other equally unobtrusive signs that can be seen by scrutinizing certain folios contained in the box. I soon come to believe that *Le Lac* might have been an injunction: do not keep. Fit for the Lake. For drowning. Into the lake it goes! I ponder that Lac: the three-letter inscription *stands out* it seems to me – like a flake, a dancer stood proud from the floor of the text –, maybe a suggestion made to the crude larva enclosed in my hand to drop head first into the lake.

I see it as black. I see it as a foundling – that's how it is for all foundlings, a hole is left, an irreparable lacuna in the soul,

116

such that however 'found' the child may be, all that's there in the home remain for it forever untraceable.

It is becoming urgent that I see this Book.

(On 20 July I find, *by chance*, when several reams of manu-scripts fall on the floor of my study, amongst the strewn sheets, a bit of paper attached to the top of a story in the far corner of the rectangle, above the spot for the title a strange mark – it's a tight scribble, in the shape of a square, in pencil, obviously intended to conceal, without destroying it, an almost invisible clue. This trace of a cancellable cancellation – a scoring through, in pencil, is easily erased – this cancella-tion that may be cancelled out necessarily arouses curiosity. I can see that this is the model on a smaller scale for what J. D. will always have called 'crypt'. Through the bars you *see* what you can't see. You see that you don't see. I am tempted to reach for the rubber. I don't. All this is sacred. All this calls for an interpretation. Interpretation is naturally equivocal, it is a true interpretation – reversible, revolving, deceptive, with the hidden truth at the heart of the scene. All this is J. D. I say to myself: the veiled seal. I 'see' illegibly. Wished I to see? Yesno. I try on the *idea* of a rubber. A sensation of irreversible sin takes hold of me. I try to examine the invisible characters of the vellum which, held up to the fire, in a saucepan held over a stove of lit coals, allows the characters traced between the death's head and the kid to show through in red. As a saucepan, I use the *strength of the midday sun*. Within a few moments, through the pencil's veil, with an inexpressible joy says William Legrand, I do not see, I do not see the first signs, I do not see but I can *make out* the following words: *we'll/keep/ it*. Appearing in blue, in J. D.'s writing. We'll keep *it* – Will we have kept it? Then no? yesno? It – is it in the book? In the end the stubborn and uneasy theme of the child found

117

and yet still enigmatically untraceable now has the enigmatic and gleaming force at the heart of the quartet. Before, I did not want to know it, now without knowing it I shall want to love it.

♩

7

Here I put the mystery of the *number* 7: the beauty of the whistle of a passing train two kilometres away must not be lost, at least for a time, amid the rumbling of an aeroplane two thousand metres away, for in the fantastical rivalry played out between the two sources of disturbance, you could almost have yourself believe that two thousand metres is a thousand times further away than two kilometres. Just as the beauty of 'we'll/keep/it', held at bay by deploying a veil that returns it to us by dint of an inaccessible of whose endurance no one can be sure, should not eclipse the charm of a 7 drawn unveiled, in the upper right corner of the first page of another story, and surrounded by a fine halo, which for all that it is more accessible, for taking place in a more rarefied, less turbulent air, is no less affecting. I will come to talk to my daughter about it just as I do of the photos, in the same breath. This 7 has something in common with the photos, I mused. It looks like J. D. There are some photos of Us, yet another story . . . I say. We are sweet as angels I say, inaccessible to the infernal swamps that seethed, it seems to me, in those First-name days. Once sorted, I list the box's golds as follows: we find six lovely old photos; a large sheet of card into which was crammed a story in surprisingly grown-up handwriting whose author is my daughter as a six-year-old little girl; I also make this unsettling discovery: everything suggests, I say, that an HC which is to say another HC, a paleonym, must

have 'given' (this word may be replaced: deposited, abandoned, fled, entrusted, etc.) J. D. other things, bodies, whose
heads and sexes were either not yet formed, or else separated.
Everything suggests that it was he and not HC who is not
me at all who will have *ciphered* the dislocated dismembered
mislaid, brought back to their senses, I say to my daughter.
Disinfected by his 7. 'For me,' I say, 'the object was decided
by him: judged, sewn up, acquitted. It's unbelievable all the
same,' I say. 'It just goes to show,' I say. 'It shows,' I say, 'what
an obscure, fearful, repelling, or desperate relationship I had
to it, object P.' Or maybe the opposite. 'From the moment
you start numbering you've already entered into reflexivity,'
says my daughter, 'you are already thinking in terms of being
read by someone else,' she says. 'Worst of all,' I say, 'is being
one's own reader, so I will have been spared the worst. You
won't say anything about what I am telling you?' I say. 'I
won't say anything,' says my daughter. 'I didn't say: you won't
say,' I say. 'I said: you won't forget.' I say. I remember that
I was always saying to her: forget. You'll forget. As for him: I
cannot command forgetting. Perhaps I gave him these things
to forget, I say to myself. No one will ever know, I say. All that
we know is error. All that we think we know is just a mixture
of error and illusion. Take Heathcliff – no one will ever have
known in the end what he will have been. A case of beget-
ting by Hallucination. All this is a fiction, I say. As if it were
my dead father who had written to me. As if it were my dead
son who had written to me. That happens. Neither man nor
woman. Neither pre-man nor pre-son. A writer? A righter?
A remover. No one will ever be able to *identify God*, said J. D.

PART II

I BRING BACK *LE PRÉNOM DE DIEU*

By now the Book-that-I-would-never-have-been-able-to-read was haunting me. In the end, it will have had to return from the night, I saw it as small and yellow, carrying the huge ball of the sun in its limbs like its own egg, and each time as if in a dream, when I am supposed to be reborn out of my own decomposition, I approach the last three steps, a paralysis takes hold of my legs, I carry around my heart a pain of immense weight, this weakness is my secret, my hidden ill, everyone but me is able to climb, behind me the crowd grows impatient: 'Move! Move!' I grab my left leg with both hands, it weighs heavy as a dead tree, it means that a part of me lies aground, a part of me hauls. The Book was not on my shelves. It is not in the house. It is entirely impossible for it ever to be in my home. That book has always been outside of itself. I am insentient. I feel not a thing upon *saying* that I know not the first thing about it. Anyone might think I am making this up. That book was always outside of me. I was always against the idea that it might insinuate itself under my roof. Besides, it *was-only-ever-there-in-my-absence*. Although I have absolutely no memory of the inside of the book, nor really of the title, I have very precise memories of my taking flight and horror. Another day in 1990, on 12 February as by chance I had noted in my notebook for that year, my friend J. D. had started talking to me about the Other, which is to say the Book. No one will believe what a dreadful day that was, trying to listen without hearing, by attempting to muffle all my senses, after which I come to escape reality: I managed to slip under the table, to place my mind in deafness, the danger passes by skimming my hair, and I awaited the end of the voice like a divine storm, with my fingers in my ears.

I look at 'it' *from afar* – as my mother with her spyglass does the geranium –, and from this distance the *Lac* looks to me like a little sparkling insect, at such a distance from me that it cannot appear to be by me. How can it be that I have no memory of it? Now this word gleams like a crown on no body. A moment later it is null and as if demagnetized. I had a narrow escape, I said to myself.

I have the dreaded book brought to me – I do not doubt for a minute that my friend E. R. has a copy. She says that she has read all the books and I believe her.

One of the effects produced by the 'search', at the frontier, for the runaway Book (you never know whom you're running from, you follow what you're running from to the point of exhaustion) is the discord (internal) the revulsion (internal). It is an extremely violent but non-externalized affect. Fear takes shape in the corners of the mouth. A crime has occurred. It's not me who wrote that, I thought. Could it be the Crime? 'Up above and on the horizon, the heavens wan ("Can you hear *heavens won*," says Henry. "Hello? Can you hear me?" "I'm doing everything I can," I say from within the fog of enigma), one heaven,' says Henry, 'and on the horizon with the blue rendings left by the forbidden Crime.'

Poe, said I-she, I have never left him. I have always needed to shudder, it's natural, I say to Henry. My children too, I made them shudder Poe. The enchanter of tombs. The patroller of ruins. Your teeth chatter, you don your paper armour, you're a little boy playing amongst the ruins, how-ever girl you may be. Henry too is a born shudderer. We patrol the lips of the abyss, we cannot help ourselves. All of a sudden I bolt, the fear gives me wings, I am in a hurry – I *am* going to miss the train that I fear taking, I *am* going to arrive late for my own lecture, in my haste to arrive *in time*, but time is not a place, there is no place but nowhere, you arrive in bad time, and with no money, no telephone alas with no memory of the phone number for life. How I shall cling to Dupin now, as if to a saviour! What if Dupin were someone else? But so reassuring, so thorough, so frightening. So imposing. Where is Dupin? On the rue Morgue. Where's that? I pleaded. Near the Opera, a little street between Big Sur church and the Martello Tower. A moment later it comes back to me.

It happened strangely between Jeffers alias Joyce and Joyce alias Joyce, a narrow passageway between two towers, and that's where I went to lose myself with Gregor. On the rue Morgue. That's a street that's tricky to find, in spite of all the instructions. I end up resolving to use the Internet – I only do so at the last Extremity. The server replies: 'we have been unable to find the address rue Morgue in the city of Paris, France' in lower case except Paris France which remain findable. In truth I tell myself I have got the wrong address. What I'm looking for – and perhaps *who* I'm looking for – perhaps 'the writer' – who has left so many traces, if anywhere at all, must be not in Paris nor in Dublin, nor in New York, not in Buffalo, not in Big Sur, but at the *Point of Departure*.

One of the effects of the sly, invisible, indescribable resistance of the Book-that-is-nowhere-to-be-found is well known – the person looking is spurred on. They cannot stop looking, for the object's *morgue* arouses an indefatigable obstinacy in the seeker. Just look, in *Angélique*, the 'Journey in search of a unique book' (Frankfurt–Paris–Vienna, the Richelieu national library, Alexandria), at the inspection of the letter *D* in the various series of catalogues of all the libraries of the world, we find Nerval in Washington, and the whole thing ends up, as you come to expect, after a double murder, in the archives of a court. Then the Bibliothèque Mazarine. Then the Bibliothèque de l'Arsenal filled with sad memories and ghosts. From there to the Archives de France, from there to the library at Compiègne. That's where the curator shows the seeker a collection of songs set to music by Rousseau, and in his handwriting, of which the first seems to be addressed to me – says Nerval:

I am not the man I once was
I shall never be myself again
My sweet summer and spring
Have fled through the window, etc.

This prompts him to return to Paris via Ermenonville, or the window.

The Ghost

In the large-format Petit Larousse, a volume that I never consult because it is too heavy to use ordinarily, I find the twinned photographs of Kafka and Kadhafi.[9] I admire the dream's mischievous powers. The king of juxtaposition. I'm not keen on the coupling. Later in the week I notice the wandering persistence of the coupling in my study. The two-headed image flaps its wings like a nocturnal sphinx at my window. *A moth*, I say to myself in English. I bat the moth-thing away. Curiosity tells me to perform the perverse, or ridiculous, action of consulting the impossible Larousse, heavy as a tombstone, at *ka*. I find side by side the effigies of Kafka and Kadhafi, or the other way around, of Kadhafi and Kafka. The two figures are captured on two parallel axes like the two symmetrical drawings on the wings of the death's head moth *Acherontia atropos*. And so my dream was not dreaming. A note of displeasure brushes, in which crease I don't know, against a bare arm of my memory which hurriedly recoils, in fright at possible contact. I would sooner forget it. The thing offers vague resistance. A bitter stupor takes hold in my mind. The double creature persists, insists. I throw it out. It comes back. I lay down the names on a purple post-it. 'Kafka and

---

[9] The name Gaddafi is transliterated as 'Kadhafi' in French.

128

Kadhafi', I write. Then I lose it. All this happens in the space of a month. As soon as I've managed to forget, the K. and K. post-it reappears. (I notice on reflection that the report laid down here used a singular. This I find interesting. K. and K. would then be perceived as one, both heads Emanated from the brain of some employee at the service of an institution or bureaucracy whose offices are camouflaged, as one might expect.) This kind of arrangement cannot go unnoticed. Or else it slips violently into the realm of the unnoticed. I imagine the Employee's ancient morgue. Someone – no one knows who – looks a prisoner up and down, someone scorns someone, someone is looked down upon as a dead man is looked at. An explanation is demanded. I throw the post-it away. I really don't know at all how I can see it holding fast by one corner onto the edge of my desk on the lower right-hand corner. Like a demon's signature, I say to myself, naturally at that time, on that day, 24 July, I can tell myself this because I don't believe in it, in the small hours that precede daylight, without fail, I am surrounded by reality, everything is in order, the succession of birds taking their first song clocks the world, I climb the ladder of minutes at the sun's slow and triumphant pace, leaving a few hours away terrors and *Acheronta atropos*. I glance at the purple post-it quivering in the corner of the sheet of white wood on the desk. I am surprised. Something surprises me. It looks blank. I check. It is. I'd rather not think. Nonetheless I decide to do away with the carrousel of signs. It seems to me that it's when I manage to get the sun to come up that at that same moment up comes the idea that this series of *little disappearances appearances* is quite William Wilson.

Note on William Wilson (a pseudonym)

William Wilson seems to be *malice incarnate* to William Wilson (that is, the homonym to his homonym, that is, he

129

who was first to enter the top left-hand corner of the page and who reports the unpleasant surprise that he feels when he meets another student, the subject of my sentence, who not only resists his tyrannical temperament (his own), not only instils in him the worrying sense that he is, he that is to say the other, easily his equal in genius, in talent, in energy, and this without effort, but more than this finds himself bearing the name of William Wilson, he too, like him, and even the same elegantly cut coat as him. You can understand, merely by looking at it from the analyst's point of view, that William Wilson, who seems to lack the kind of ambition that drives William Wilson to dominate all his fellows, including William Wilson, might appear malicious to William Wilson, because – in a society of young men where it is customary to practise rivalry, impertinence, where it is seemly to strut, to gainsay, to mortify, instead of serving up aggressive platitudes, the scoffing and provocations to which all have grown used – he allows himself to behave with true dignity and to counter through kindness, he William Wilson, his fury and brutal – even disloyal – behaviour, that of William Wilson. It is almost hatred.

And with this, what sends William Wilson wild with rage, is that when, after five years of exasperation in the same establishment, he at last goes somewhere new, which enables him to relegate this episode of excessive homonymy to oblivion, only three years pass before the other William Wilson resurfaces. The pattern of these eclipses-returns is between three and five years. But it is not long before William Wilson can no longer shake off a sense of William Wilson's imminent presence. Everything in William Wilson's tempestuous life is as if William Wilson, instead of being the upstanding, gifted, virtuous young man that he will always have been, were but the atrocity of a conscience, a spectre walking the inner path of William Wilson, and all this owing to a homonymy and a large number of coincidences (appearance, date of birth, etc.)

One night, William Wilson even comes uncannily to resemble William Wilson, or at least William Wilson convinces himself of an inexplicable resemblance when, bent over William Wilson fast asleep – over whose face he shines a bright light –, he thinks he sees, he sees only his features, the features of the sleeper, which are *his*, are not his, but to his great horror his.

But in the case of K. and K., you only have to take a brief glance at the astounding coupling that is framed on the page such that nothing separates the two figures, to be sent reeling: the one is undoubtedly the other's *exact* stranger. The two gazes are inseparable.

ANOTHER WILLIAM

'Do you remember the name of the narrator of *The Purloined Letter*?' I say to my daughter. And while she's thinking I take another step: 'He's called William.' 'Oh yes, so he is,' says my daughter. That makes one more William, I say to myself. There are just as many Williams as we might imagine, as a first name for a Spectre – that is, as Poe thinks, for a *conscience*, 'William' will do as a signature for anyone meaning to let the other sign in his place. Why are they called William? I was going to ask, when my daughter, who reads my mind as Dupin does the narrator's, replies, before I could finish my thought: it's because of *Will I am*. No one could say otherwise. Another William – I make a note, as a specialist in literary research. A detective is a detective right down to his very soul, as the master William Dupin is for eternity. I have noticed that research is in truth most often guided by a series of aberrations. It has to be said that Secrets – those fantastical creatures that reign over our destinies, and which lead us along blindfolded, our breast pierced with the thorns of despair

– are beings-things whose strength lies in the inexhaustible production of semblances. Such semblances are true hints. It would be a mistake not to take even the most grotesque and implausible of skits seriously. For example this business, worthy of *Atreus and Thyestes* (a scandal sheet specializing in the most improbable, the most extreme news items, I have in mind cases of cannibalism leading to a person eating their own flesh, etc.), the pairing of K. and K. as incompatible in one of the rooms of the house of Larousse. These distasteful performances that induce an effect of *dogged indifference*, a sharp flinching movement, all the familiar signs of revulsion, hold in truth an unaccountable fascination for the audience, who find themselves, as a result, divided within themselves and a little treacherous. Never mind all that. I say to myself. Carried away by the investigative impulse, I check that Dupin's double, the friend, the witness, the biographer, the second – or the first – of the *two madmen*, his other, and his same, Dupin *bis*, is also called William no less, that's right. The investigator in the affair of *The Murders in the Rue Morgue*, which forever marked my childhood imagination with its double claw, the reasoner who *demonstrates impossibility* by demonstrating that every impossibility has its opposite double, that is, its secret possibility, and who affectionately mocks his defective double, the prefect of police, the bungling analyst who is nonetheless allowed *the last words* of this long nightmarish autopsy, quoted by our Dupin, I mean the famous phrase: *I mean the way he has 'de nier ce qui est, et d'expliquer ce qui n'est pas'*[10] is also a William.

Those two make for quite a pair of madmen, and we see William *falling* into Dupin's bizarreries, in the downwards arc of a determined fall, for it is always thus in cases of pos-

---

[10] 'To deny what exists and to explain what doesn't.'

session by a double, by virtue of *the accident of our both being in search of the same very rare and remarkable volume*. As soon as two dreamers coming from two apparently foreign points of departure are looking at the same time for *the same volume*, very rare and remarkable, it is only to be expected that each should *entitle* the other to his confidences. Such is life in unity of internal objects. You make night day and you nocturnalize the night twenty-four hours a day. We no longer know who of us two says who writes what the other thinks he is saying:

> *the accident brought us into closer communion. We saw each other again and again. Such that we became one. Seeking in Paris the objects I then sought, I felt the society of such a man would be to me a treasure beyond price; and this feeling I frankly confided to him.*

> *Had the routine of our life at this place been known to the world, we should have been regarded as madmen – although, perhaps, as madmen of a harmless nature. Our seclusion was perfect. We admitted no visitors. Indeed the locality of our retirement had been carefully kept a secret from my own former associates; and it had been many years since Dupin had ceased to know or be known in Paris. We existed within ourselves alone.*

> *It was a freak of fancy in my friend (for what else shall I call it?) to be enamored of the Night for her own sake; and into this bizarre-rie, as into all his others, I quietly fell; giving myself up to his wild whims with a perfect abandon.*

I am quoting from 'memory'.

When I see that we are all of us double, that even the most singular of analysts cannot do without and could not be without the shadow of himself, and that even a sage can only be so by being two sages, a madman is always two madmen, I invariably think of Gregor, only to instantly forget him, such that he vanishes like a dream behind the horizon. I forgot him again only last night.

It occurs to me that I have never forgotten anyone as frequently and as precipitately as Gregor. I have a hurried and mechanical way of shooing him off, without losing a tenth of a second. The moment I saw that bundle of letters lurking behind a sheet of blue card at the bottom of the Box, I took out all the manuscripts and papers packed on top of those ruins and I shut up the Box. But the sheet of blue card had marked out the manuscripts. Behind this covering you couldn't see them – these letters, that is. Unlike the prefect of police I do not deny what is, but it is not always so simple to affirm that what is is what one might call *is*. Gregor, is it? Is he? I believed so. Once. For one interminable year. Until the day when, having ceased to be what he passed for being, it became something entirely other. I don't deny that this Once, objectively such, is not like other onces, which display all the features that distance renders indistinct, which are pale, disembodied and dried up. This Once will not hold still. It still has a grip on the present by one tooth, which will not fall out. Most of all by one letter. I myself had contrived not to know that there was buried in the earth of my texts a veritable mine of G., I think. When J. D. brought it to light, in the treatise *Geneses, Genealogies, Genres, and Genius* published in 2002, it became more and more impossible – because there are numerous degrees to the impossible – to protect myself against the dangers of what I from then on referred to, after J. D.'s discovery, as the *G-hosting*. Not that the strength of my refusal weakened. But the objective strength of the G-force increased. You realize that when a letter has a mind to propa-

136

gate itself, it's easy: it has numerous contaminable regions at its disposal since it can play on registers of sounds and slip in beneath a host of homophonic equivalents. Avoiding G. would mean no longer saying genie, genius, genealogy etc. etc. and yet in so saying I greatly simplify. I have an obscure sense that it's *the fear of this fear* that I fled the day J. D. spoke in front of me and for me of his reading of *Prénom de Dieu*.

It was that, the very same, or more or less, that made me bristle the time when I *fell into* the bizarrerie of the K. and K. coupling which I took to be an attack aimed at me by the house of Larousse. I give no credence to the innocence of the famous image *Clerk*. And if I am the only one to have such a deep-felt reaction, it is because that blow – the *g*-emination of *Kafka* and *Kadhafi* – was struck at my self.

I am losing my way by all appearances. Even as I lose myself in the labyrinth of an unbroken night, and so in suffering the anxieties that accompany the movements I make still in the direction of what escapes from the Box, I recognize the ancient syntax of my terrors. When I speak of the extraordinary case of Kadhafi and Kafka for me what we have here is an act of coupling committed by the demon of perversity. There is no telling which is the Foreign Body for the other. Some readers of the Larousse are on the side of Kadhafi. Some are on that of Kafka. There is a stock of great suffering in that. No one can bind K. and K., that is, K. with K. or K. as K., K. to K., without loss of life. One is the negation of the other 'in reality'. And yet, you can imagine that in certain dreams one might act as a mask for the other. That will have been able to happen to me. That will only have been able to happen to me to the extent that Kafka, for reasons that have yet to be revealed to me, might be Kadhafiable. I note that I react to this apparition, institutionalized, and poisoned by laroussian perversity to which the finger has yet to be pointed, with the extreme repugnance that Perseus shows for the Medusa who is horrified at the sight of the elegant mask of her murder. It is the same chill that takes hold of William Wilson upon seeing that William Wilson close to. Is it not dreadful to be condemned to admit a visible kinship with one's own murderer? I mean one's own victim. I cannot hate my neighbour my brother without being hated myself

Imagine now that a substitution occurs between a tyrant and a poet. It has been known. Both of them, K. and K., are specialists of despotism. Persecution holds no secrets for them. We cannot imagine, though we must, the force of attraction exerted by the foreigner upon the foreigner, the opposite upon the opposite, K. upon K., William upon William, and which can only come from a secret source, namely the intuition of a shared taste for a unique book both untraceable and sought.

Now imagine that there lies hidden in Kafka, behind the appearance, the figure, in the letters of Kafka, a student who had undertaken the same studies as William Wilson, and who had quickly become a poet of the bizarreries and inner disarray very much like the oddities of Kafka, who had stolen under cover of night into Kafka's thoughts, whom Kafka could have several times met in the stairwell of the building, with the strange sensation of happening upon himself, and who turns out to be irksome, belligerent, troublesome or troubled perhaps, such that they come to blows. In the end he wins. All that is not a real fiction, it is a fiction that happened in reality. Gregor had done exactly as K. did with Kafka. He had infiltrated Kafka then he absorbed Kafka body and soul and he became him. There is no making judgements on an act of *spiritual* cannibalism. Is it a crime or a religion? According to Henry, what with Kafka having been eaten dead by Gregor in 1964 then *brought up* by Gregor in 1965, this eating could even be considered an excess of admiration. A tape worm, says Henry. I would have said an *uroboros* snake. But re-call is what I'm avoiding.

Yes, I realize the detour I have to make to get back to the bottom of the Box, on this day, 24 July, a year has gone by as deep as the reading of a *Tale of Mystery and Imagination*, in the bowels of mysteries you don't notice the time rolling by. My mother is assiduously reading a unique and rare book introduced to her by me, under different titles, and it's still on the same page the same story of the *expedition to the P. D.* In the end we go around the world in eighty metres, she sets sail weakly towards its horizon, the crossing demands all of my mother's gathered strength. I look at the garden from her point of view: it grows vast. Suddenly I understand the jungly hugeness of a red geranium. I had forgotten old age but now it's back. 'I'm not a burden to you?' says my mother on 24 July. It hadn't occurred to me that my mother could think that I could think that. 'You're a delight,' I say and I gaze at the thing of exquisite peculiarity that is her face – a furrowed landscape, stained, strewn with white tufts where two tiny wedding torches have been lit. 'It's the box that's a burden.' Start out from the Box to reach the *P. D.*: a few steps, but which offer a resistance that's unshakable because it's internal. If one day I manage ten centimetres, a frost takes hold of me, my temperature drops to 34.8°, our legs are like ice cubes, the Pole of the Last Extremity will not be conquered without a fight. When will I be able to say to myself: 'at last the last page has been read'? Because it is not I who am leading this battle, it's the forces of the Book-that-cannot-be-read. I am not crossing the little study whose door fifty centimetres from my chair gives out onto the landing where the cupboard, the box's mausoleum, huddles, but a long, colourless corridor that leads to the monumental entrance of a large library. I cannot believe that this airlock is 'the past'. Such a close proximity of the most foreign entity I have ever known. Such a little square where the thick, hurried volumes of *oblivion* are stacked. Poe's arrival here, on 24 July, comes as no surprise.

No, there is no more powerful, more active, more dynamic and insidious, more relentless Worm than the earthworm called *Oblivion*. If you imagine for this red Worm some dreams for it to devour, it swells the box and you can no longer make out the edges.

The Serpent Oblivion devours my lions one after the other. Sated. What's left is the Serpent full of lions. When will the Serpent's Serpent come? At the end of death when the dead are dead, says Poe to Baudelaire, the teeth are left. As soon as you are foolhardy enough to think of them, they rise up and bite.

'I've always felt that Poe's spirit-jaw was mixed up in all my chapters,' says the Book, right from the foreword, it was already his cold breath and above all his voice that I could hear calling me by a name that was not yet mine, says the Book, this voice recognizable in amongst all others, as you know, which is barely a voice, a veiled whispering that reaches us exhausted from having had to travel the length of the Acheron's gorges, all breath weighed down by this journey, a wail but penetrating, and therefore irresistible.

One night I hear the Box whistle, a whispering telephones me, I quickly get up, in the dark you can cover huge ground, I can clearly hear the Box quietly panting the first syllable of my first name: 'Hé! Hé!' alas, how distressing, I know of no sadder song. 'I'm coming! I'm coming!' I cried, 'I'm co . . .' He hung up. *He* hung up. Ah! What an air of reproach is blowing, in front of the cupboard, in the corner of the cupboard, beneath the lowest shelf.

A fright rings me up in the middle of the night. I wake up with a start. The sentence moans: *'It's been months now!'* The whole agony of the vanquished invalid is intoned here. Who? Someone is complaining, to me, in me, about me, me, someone is lamenting their having to wait for some communication with life for months now. All of a sudden I come back up to the surface of common tenses. Oh, what terrifying force that verb *to be* has! By whom have these months *been*?, I feared, is that me? Ah, I can feel that I have committed a huge and long sin, I have left out life, I have left off all love of its fidelity, it's un-been me, shows itself to be the runaway boy playing amongst the ruins of Proust, so can one *forget* one's grandmother? deny her? go so far as to make a desert the size of a province, lose her in a forest without even noticing? I *want* to call you, suddenly I am all of me no more than the pillar of fire of this *I Want*. I Want to be the caller graced, but will the crime I have committed prevent me from being so? Now that it's been *months* since I called you, where did I have the dreams? a six-month-long wall, six monstrous unities of alienation, now stands between my furious desire and all my archives. For all my pleas, your number has stayed where I left it the last time, and since then *It* has made an impassable band of time. Ovid, help me, make me into a bird, a fairy. Ovid too has kept back. Eurydice is angry. I have forgotten her number! She doesn't pick up. Will she never again answer me? Naturally Eurydice is not her real name. I have never uttered your true name. We sit down in the dust. We cover our heads with ashes. We do not understand each other. It's been months. We have managed to pass through this stretch of life without talking to life, without calling it. We don't even know when we forgot it. Is there such a thing as months that are not months but great holes the size of whole neighbourhoods in the existence of God?

When Marcel suddenly realizes that *it's been months* since he remembered to dream about his grandmother he wants to die. I want to telephone her, he notes, in his coloured notebook, but for not having called her in months, time has got hold of and destroyed all the numbers after the dial code. How quickly the vulture cleans up! All that's left of the adored magic formula is the first three letters GUT to mock my suffering. I search in vain for the numbers that were my life's song in my memory, but the sweet music has died out. All that remains of her num- are these three bodiless letters. *It's been months*. I don't deny what is: a six-month nothingness is a double murder. I search out my address books. I find the red one. There is a number there on the left that I recognize – it's the one that You gave me when you came out of hospital, I had doubted your resurrection, the number of a day, for a day, now lost, gone, erased – both the number and the day. Ruin has half-eaten it. I have lost the last digits, I

143

think your number was pink. I am in desperation and pain. I hunt for the black book in vain, and when I reach the limit of despair, I am going to die. In vain in vain, Françoise arrives. I hurry to her, I speak into her ear, do you remember God's number? I quietly yelled. '*That's all* that's got you into this state?' '*That'sall!!*' She speaks loudly. As if this whole scene were not under the orders of death. But of course I've got it. She is going to give it to me. So there is a gentle and ordinary world where the staff remain intact and have nothing to fear from the rages of the dead. *She* has the number for God-night and terror. *Be quiet!* I whispered. I don't want us overheard. This is only too obvious to me, my only chance of *survival*, if I should fail, if You don't speak to me, if You reject me, if You don't forgive me for having *forgotten* to call you for months, if you don't absolve me for this monstrous Delay, there will be *no witness*. And so if *You* don't answer the phone, there will be nothing else for it but to carry on as if *nothing* had happened, ever. Then see later if I can live amongst ruins. She's got it! The number! God's first name written out to the letter! At least the horror of forgetting will find a limit. Glimmer! God grows back in a neighbouring garden, if not in mine.

Even if we forgot that we forgot, if we only forgot, that would be nothing at all, it would be just fine. But forgetting won't let itself be forgotten.

Here is where I'm putting, so as not to forget it, this chapter buckling under the horror of forgetting, of not forgetting, of never being able to forget that we have forgotten, of being unable to forget forgetting.

When we say that we have forgotten, we demand acquittal, we do not forget ourselves, we say 'it is the other who has let themselves be forgotten', the grandmother has passed away, we did nothing. And then there have been months of forgetting that become impassable.

To get back to the Box: had I *consecrated* it to Oblivion? Was this a conditional concession? In perpetuity? Had I entrusted it to the River? Then washed my hands in it? I'll not think of it anymore. I'll notthink of it more and more. Such that the Box remains. Perfectly forgotten. Remains. Is. Again. The difference between the inert thing that it was and what it 'is' is that it *is* now. Active with a sly, unpredictable activity. It's that, at night, no doubt about it, that administers dreams to me peopled with importunate missing persons, ancient outcasts who wander my streets naked.

Today I notice, I noted on 1 August, that my instinct has been telling me for weeks to *reduce* the Book to its initials, so I shrink it down, I preserve it in the form of the initials *P. D.* out of a taste for the chemical formula, I say to myself. It is now that, thanks to one of those strokes of luck that make up the event in the *Tales of the Utmost Mystery and Imagination*, I discern a clue that had thus far escaped me in my adherence to the title's first reading. Thanks to an oversight – if there is such thing as involuntary inattention by that name – instead of *Prénom de Dieu* I think I can make out: *Point of Departure*. Coincidence and synonymy.

And so the most distant part of my life, and which I no longer like at all, not even, which no longer even seems to be my life but rather the rough draft of a story that remained unfinished, because inaccurate, made up, which I could describe as the First Extremity, it's at this point that it will have taken over a whole part of my real life, in which I see it occupying the all-important place of *Point of Departure*. And yet I had lived confident that it was as if it had never existed. 'I have only ever begun writing,' I have always said to Henry, '*after* the departure.' In the end I always write after the departure. All the people are already gone. Wait for me! I shouted. They are far away. The world is a scattering of lifeless objects, 'my things', innumerable futilities, that I try to gather up instead of starting to run with everything I've got to catch up with the others. And I am no more than a remainder that cries out amongst a field of mute remains. I am not there to begin with. I feel like I am.

But who?

Be brave, I tell myself. You have to *dive in*, says Marcel the seeker. 'Maybe I'm the madman.' I didn't want to tell myself that. Is that the reason, too shameful to admit, why I haven't thrown the Box away? The effort I'm making now to keep hold of the thread of the hypothesis surpasses the heart of the teller. (1) I admit that someone in me didn't want to *lose the madman*. (2) I admit to an extraordinary lack of courage for crossing the passage full of horrors and humility that will bind me to the moment that precedes the truth. (I'll finish these confessions off later.) (3) These are perhaps the reasons why I was scared when J. D. drew close to the *fire* – for him it was paper. But wouldn't that paper warmed by his touch reveal some dreaded signature? I am afraid he'll see what I was afraid to see and, worst of all, that he not be afraid. Or else, that he be afraid. I said to myself. Wherever I turn lies terror, and murder.

As for the inner book ('the trickiest to decipher', as Henry says), might mine have had a double? Now I suspect my *first* horror book of having been *The Murders in the Rue Morgue*. I've never read it. As soon as the door was open, I was in the mouth of the story, swallowed, crushed between its jaws, gobbled up. This story is an Ourang-Outang. It's no use resenting him for the violence he does us. We have taught him how to use a razor blade, and he wields it to shave away at our hearts. The man who is a shadow of a man, the entirely innocent convict, he whom we cannot resent for tearing us limb from limb, for slitting our throats, for forcing us upside down up into the chimney, our extranatural hero, is this Story to which I drew closer, towards which I was drawn by my fate, I was 11 years old, when it was all over I went to see it at the zoological gardens, we all bore the scars, I clung onto the bars of the book, I stared at it in this barred proximity, I contemplated its very pale eyes behind which the Unexplained lay sleeping for eternity. It was a neutral, decommissioned pity for us all – those killed, the killers, the prisoners, those driven mad by madness, those by unmadness, a soapwashed, disinfected pity enclosed us. Once the passion passed.

I started again. I closed in. And everything was instantly guilty and innocent. Ourang and Outang. What's trickiest to decipher is the force of the force of attraction that has always commanded me not to shy away from the unfathomable, excessively bright gaze of the Highly-powerful. In the end, will I, consciously, have read the Story that nonetheless *was read*? For it was read by someone (in me) who had the strength that I have not. When it is all over, we shut the innocent monster up in a big zoological box.

Ah! I can see it, I have for the Box the ancient flame of terror that quakes before the Ourang-Outang. What if it still had claws, after all this time?

⁊

At that moment, a sort of vague and embryonic conception of Dupin's thinking enters mine: I feel like I am on the border of understanding without being able to understand. If I follow all the characters featured in my Inner Book, then the whole business of the metamorphosis of G. G. would be a reproduction of the Poe story up on which as a child I crept, hiding behind Baudelaire and shaking like a leaf.

The texts are discovered headless. At the bottom of the chest lies the head-eater: Gregor. He signs himself G. G. What is left of the Ourang-Outang the great beast of the islands of east India. Eater and eaten will have been shut up in the same chest, I say to myself. Between the letters of the Ourang-Outang and the manuscripts of P. D. lies a layer of unyielding oblivion.

Were these texts written in the era G. G. or after G. G.? In spite of G. G.? Or according to G. G.? Are the headless texts malgregorian? Demonized or exorcized? No reply. J. D. had cast upon the decapitated the names that calm. But when it comes to the Inner Book no one can help us with a single rule, Henry tells me. What about G. G.'s letters? Why not thrown away? They have slivers of raw flesh between their lines.

What I had never wanted to think about since the Box were its depths, I say to myself. Its depths are the madman.

149

We don't want to lose the Ourang-Outang, nor keep it. We did love it, but we can't remember. But something in the extreme transparency of its light eyes makes us want to cry. It's an absence of shade, a lack of worry. The frightening unmoving limpidity of the gaze that knows nothing of regret.

As I saw William Legrand being made to do, I warm up the trail again and soon the name *Gregor* turns reddening into *Gorger*. This reading is only too true. In a certain way, the dreamer tells me, Gregor has haunted us thus far, until today, until this page, he has swallowed us and I have swallowed him, I myself even have perhaps gorged myself on Gregor's remains. I can no more think that when I am in my right mind than I can utter the name of the Ourang-Outang. I always point to it via a detour or by a metaphor.

In the Box, the little photo of G. G., passport-sized. If I say now that I see Gregor as having the same face as Edgar Poe, no one will believe me. It is the same disquieting gaze, that's never lowered, that remains. When I turn back to Henry, he is surprised. Well well, a photo of Poe without his moustache! A curiosity. At last, I start having doubts.

§

I am not the only one to be always attended by a small and spectral company of doubts. Usually, someone who never goes anywhere without these guardians, these safety rails, who, never sleeping, are quite reassuring but burdensome too, who upset our inner peace, tug at our sleeves, whisper sceptical commentaries on anything and everything, would most likely take care not to mention this state of mind. But not always. I know of one, *l'aq.* Meryon, who was not afraid to frankly air his concerns to Baudelaire: 'Dear Charles, tell me, *do you believe* in the reality of this Edgar Poe. Charles', he will have written, from Charles to Charles, Charles Meryon the *aquatinter*, author of strange Parisian scenes whose tumultuous skies heavy with wrath and malice line the mind of the other Charles. The bell towers point them towards this sky. The two Charleses meet and mingle by Gare Saint-Lazare. Each Charles projects onto the impressionable mind of the neighbouring Charles reveries of twenty lines about powerful fantastical engravings. The visions and reveries grow drunk on the same melancholy.

Naturally Baudelaire, this is on 8 January 1860, replies by return letter. He affirms that he is well placed to know that *this Edgar Poe has some reality*, since he has been translating him for years. We can understand that Meryon might have had his concerns about the quality of the reality of the evidence offered by Baudelaire. The truth is that Baudelaire never set eyes on Edgar Poe. Just as 'Edgar Poe', if he ever existed in reality, never set foot in Paris, something that no reader could ever have suspected, following Dupin and his friend William, eyes shut through the streets of Saint-Germain or around the Opéra. For his part, Meryon has good reason for thinking that Edgar Poe is the pseudonym of a society of highly deft and highly powerful writers-imitators, whom *nothing escapes*. They are everywhere, this secret society. And they only have to *copy reality so as to pass it off* as the truth of fiction. So as to have the truth pass from reality to fiction. Here's the proof: the whole story of the rue Morgue, including the Ourang-Outang, happened to the engraver, and he has witnesses. It holds up, there's no denying that his story holds water. More proof: all the murders that bring about Dupin's cases and make his name first took place in reality and are then taken up, transposed or metamorphosed by 'Edgar Poe'.

151

Such a genius is besides always a society of highly powerful writers, which recruits by all manner of underhand means. Baudelaire himself, being part of this secret society, cannot be a trustworthy witness. Although neither is there any proof that Baudelaire consciously knew of his membership of the society by the same name. For these invisible societies that exist, as Balzac will also have noted, are in truth *truly secret* societies – that is, networks that communicate by unconscious pathways. One day you discover by chance that you are a member of such a society. It is as troubling as the unexpected discovery in the hallway of a bedroom identical to your own, inhabited by a neighbour whom, having moved in at the same time as you, you hadn't noticed and whose presence you learn of the day when he mixes up the doors, and even hat stands, together with the fact that he has the same position as you at the Insurance Company. When it comes to apes, for example, there can only be one, we tell ourselves, and it's mine. Somehow I have even been known to feel bound to an Ourang-Outang as to a brutish brother or the other way around, or as to a son or a lover. Naturally I don't tell anyone. I hardly tell myself even. In the beginning all I could see was a young man of 27, with very light eyes, red hair

For me, there is no doubting that Charles – Meryon, that is – intuitively *saw* the *unbelievable* 'reality' of Edgar Poe. He 'sees' Edgar Poe as a ghost, like his characters. Such expertise in 'fiction' is all the more familiar to him for the fact that he is himself, Charles, an artist who works in ghosts, and ghosts of two types: (a) true ghosts – like his famous *Ghost Ship*, which he manages testingly to call up, for any viewer of this etching is obliged to admit that she is *seeing the invisible*; (b) ghost substitutes, like all these phantasmagorical Parisian 'landscapes', which show the City as *afflicted*, drained, tormented, by the innumerable spectres of his memory. According to

152

this Charles, *Edgar* was the anagram who *garde*, which is to say *guards*, the secret of a great absentee. When he *questions* Baudelaire, two thoughts at least haunt his sanity: Edgar Poe could be a designation of origin, controlled (by a society, for example), or *non-controlled*. He could be the ghost of an artist capable of making himself up exactly as he makes up one of his characters, all equally endowed with an unusual degree of veracity. He could in this case be a fiction *required* and engendered by the powers of fiction, a process comparable to those mechanisms of evolution brought to light by another Charles from the series of Charleses – namely, Charles Darwin. We mustn't minimize the role of these transmissions of thoughts by *letters* and names. This Meryonic thought is accompanied by a hypothesis that is plausible in reality: what if it were Charles who *made* Edgar Poe? That is to say, Baudelaire. That would explain the absolutely perfect simulation of Paris.

Charles Meryon, I'm thinking of you! I say to myself. The city changes. Paris, New York, everything turns into allegory for me, but nothing of the melancholy moves.

♪

Am I a fiction? This question, which does irreparable damage to us, is the ghost that my ghost turned, trembling, towards J. D. We await a judgement, we hope, unbelieving. Edgar Poe too, or else 'Edgar Poe', could not but tremble too – 'this Edgar Poe', the greatest of pranksters –, on the day when, as he tells us, he will have discovered the *double* of his double *Murders in the Rue Morgue*.

How to explain, wonders Edgar Poe, *the existence of another ape*, another ape man, and, even better, another writer with an ape, and exactly the same ape? My neighbour my brother, with the look of a French sailor returned from *Borneo*, ruddy face more than half hidden by red whiskers and moustache. It's impossible. Yet it is. Eugène Sue, the other one, has exactly the same ape, unfortunately equipped with the same kind of razor, who will sign the same mysterious murders. Although for Eugène Sue it is the other who is the other, obviously. According to Dupin the impossible always finds an explanation in the Inner Book.

Within every sensitive soul (sailor, poet, invalid) there is always a great ape and a tomb. As long as none tries to relieve him of his razor blade, with which he signs, the Ourang-Outang is no killer. That man is gentle as a lamb as long as we believe in *his reality*. But if anyone should suspect that there is an Ourang-Outang in him, he cuts. There is also the fable of the *Monkey Who Becomes a Writer* in La Fontaine, but the Monkey there is only a baboon. Here is where I'm putting the following coincidence: in a former life (before becoming the most impressive aq. ever to inspire Victor Hugo), we find out that Meryon, Charles, is aboard the sloop *Le Rhin* – he will have dropped anchor in Borneo and in the Polynesian islands. Numerous sketches attest to this. The man bears a curious resemblance to an ape. Charles, I mean – there's no knowing whether he drew his self-portrait accentuating the resemblance to the inner beast intentionally or unintentionally. According to Charles, his neighbour, his fellow man it is absolutely him. An unmistakable and doleful unease emanates from his face, half hidden behind bushy whiskers. This portrait *calls out* to the visitor of the Louvre picture galleries, as it called out to Baudelaire, whispering: 'Look at me, for the love of God. Do you believe in my signature?' You can see he doubts his reality. He will have drawn this pain, which is precisely his signature itself. The colour of doubt is these gradations of grey wandering amongst the blacks, of which Hugo will have wanted to be seen as the rightful heir. 'An *Ourang-outang*!! I have often been compared to an ape', whispers the letter from Charles to Charles. What he wishes for deep in his heart is for Charles to reassure him: 'No, Charles, you're no assassimian.' Unfortunately for Charles, doubt having never been lifted by one for the other, these two admirable versions of the same mishap suffered the same misfortune, from birth on the same day to burial. The brigands, the thieves who break into the house at night, the ghosts of whom you are afraid as you are getting into bed, Freud would say, Henry says, are all descended from the Ourang-Outang. We are all of us afraid of ourselves.

The strangest dream: I have climbed up a ladder to wash the windows. I am young, beautiful and nice – I gush with praise for the woman next door, of whom I cannot speak highly enough. In my arms I am holding a chimpanzee and a catgorilla. They are getting in the way of the cleaning. I thrust these apes upon the woman dreaming the dream. The catgorilla takes a real liking to her and it is very disgusting. The woman dreaming literally casts herself out of the dream through the window that I have just cleaned. And yet, I say to myself on waking, it's not disgust that I feel for G. G. But I don't know what to call the kind of highly powerful refusal that I have built up against his *false* reality.

This dream means that I would like to get rid of the madman and keep the madness, I say to myself. The idea that that would be impossible saddens me. But this desire would explain the Box.

Here is the hypothesis:

Someone – oh how it is not me – who had known a certain Gregor, a character who may have been the creation of several fraudulent literary critics of talent, a sort of Golem of the *arcane* mysteries of twentieth-century literary theory, crafted to perfection, left us this cardboard (*arca*) *chest* as a legacy. A

155

moral sense of responsibility, as unfounded as a categorical imperative, forbids us from going against the wishes of the departed. We obey the dead without knowing why. I know why: we fear the vengeance of these helpless creatures.

᧝

'Do you believe in the reality of this Gregor?' That's the question. Wait for an answer from the other end. The call doesn't get through.

Why would I inherit from this woman, I said to myself, that is, the Box full of debts? Hers. That's not my fault, I say to myself. How irritating! It is as if I had within me someone who was afraid of herself, hidden away in a mental attic, a cast-off, a character from a play that I had started writing *before* I had matured an art, a work-in-progress, such a sham as to shame. An attempted *novel*, I who never wanted to write a 'novel', with ultra-novelistic, feverish characters, memories descended from a mania that grows rough and musky on the moors, as if someone had tried to graft those raging moorlands onto a neighbourhood of the Lower East Side. What a naïve, dangerous imitation. And you don't even know that you are *in* the imitation right up until the day when the larva is found dead in the morning.

If it weren't for the *Prénom de Dieu*, I say to Henry, we wouldn't give it another thought. Unfortunately, I have totally lost all memory of the circumstances of the gestation of these objects.

The sailor, who couldn't control his Ourang-Outang, if you remember, I say to Henry, no one held him responsi-

156

ble for the murders. I don't see why I should answer for my Ourang-Outang, and yet I am sent a court summons, and I don't throw it away. Worse still, it's as if I had sent it myself. It is as if I were suffering from a violent antipathy for this person, the other woman, who enlists a homonymy to get me to take on a life that I would never have agreed to countersign. I despise the mad. How well I understand William Wilson! The real one. Since it must be pointed out that of the two William Wilsons, however apparently identical they may be when it comes to the *details*, only one has the status of truth. *This* William Wilson is the true one, whereas the one who calls himself William Wilson, even if it's not him, nor is he the *other* William Wilson: he's *an* other. We won't ever be able to pretend that the mysteries named Coincidences didn't exist. It's a Coincidence. I have no hesitation, as HC, in saying that I am on William Wilson's side in this unfortunate misadventure. I know only too well what it is to be taken for someone you aren't for the sake of a homonymy. If you share a large number of interests, the mix-up can cause real burns to the thought. If you have nothing whatever in common, it's a constant cause for offence. You are expelled from yourself, I say to Henry. You are carried off, hollowed out, switched over. You are stolen. What you are is not. What you are not is put in your place all over the place. It's not that the other one, the fake William Wilson, was mistreated, it's that I, I say, I am intimately mixed up in matters that are entirely foreign to me. I have, I say, been receiving letters in my name. I can't even talk to you about it. I can't say any more about it, even to Henry, I say to myself. Being spectralized-alive is a nightmare. Nowadays we don't even have the option of waking – nightmares are immortalized by the unlimitable resources of teletechnology. We 'live', if that may still be called 'life', on line, lives that are not ours and which have us passing impotently through stories of which we haven't the first idea *in reality*. And we will never again be able to use the expression 'in reality' *in reality*.

When did I start being author to myself? Did I write the stories of the *Prénom de Dieu* as fully responsible for my actions? Was I sunk in a state of hypnosis? Or more precisely, was *she* sunk? Who was she who said I when I knew nothing of myself? I owe this to Henry: on this day, 5 August, he points out this feature of which I have not the least recollection – that I is in the masculine in those stories. This only adds to the confusion. In my avowed books, I is always in the feminine.

Or maybe it was all written *by* dream, dreaming all the while, and what would explain the lack of head, of beginning, of ending, was the unbiddable brutality of awakenings that burst into the bedroom and proceeded to arrest he – or she – who was dreaming before they finished their burglary. All that was left was the scene of the crime, a demented disarray owing to this police's untimely entrance, and traces for which no one would be there to admit having been responsible.

I was asleep, when it happened.

I said 'burglary'. My double secret fear: being the perpetrator, not being the perpetrator of the burglary. I remember: I had *totally forgotten* the stunned expression, the uncertainty etched on J. D.'s face, that day in 1965 as he held in his hands the scruffy pile of savagely scissored sheets, of sickly bodies, which I must have placed there as one might entrust the lost patient to the hands of a shaman. He's the one who remembers. Nothing is more quickly effaced than the trace of a fatal disease upon the return from the dead except on the right bank of the Acheron. You can no longer even see the river.

The abyss has scarred over! The scar is lost in sand. I am no longer the dead person.

Had he not spoken of it again, had he not made his statement, the investigation would never have been re-opened, nor the fire re-started. I have noticed that there is only one Forgetting, you only ever really forget once. If you slash, accidentally or on purpose, the box where the past is shut up, there's no undoing what's done – the beast escapes and runs amok through the whole city. 'What's that? What's going on? What's happening to me? What sort? Who's ever going to read that? etc.' I'm quoting from his statement. It runs to several pages. It states that the manuscript that would later be called *Le Prénom de Dieu* had no name, that the thing is nonetheless a found *literary* object. A sort of wild abandoned black child. A cloud of wandering questions. The tone of bewilderment never lessens – we see the teller, overawed, trying to record all the aspects of this unease, as might the analyst concerned most of all about the future of the analysis of the moment, and to the very bottom of his heart, about the extinction of these analytical faculties: what cannot be analysed is precisely what merits analysis.

In hindsight, there is something reassuring about this taking leave of the senses. I feel less alone.

A comment to put here, 3 August, or later on:

(1) I realize, in the moment when I'm copying out a part of J. D.'s statement, that immediately after having gathered up a 'book' (not yet finished) with no name or family, he himself owned up to being the signatory of a literary 'object' of unclassifiable genre, and whose title, he says, is *unpublishable*.

Which just goes to show that *unpublishable* objects do end up being published nonetheless. That doesn't mean they have become publishable. They remain unpublishable.

(2) In his errant statement, J. D. inserts the following sentence, all on its own between two paragraphs, themselves buffeted by the unreliable elements: 'I'll have to come back to it, then. I say to myself.' Hearing that, I thought he'd said 'I have to come back to it, I say to myself.' Wait: in his written statement (though he might have changed his mind on re-reading) the sentence had wavered, snapped in two then settled around a full stop. And what might look like an opinion had become an injunction. This double sentence that I had paid no attention to suddenly takes on, as I 'read' it for the first time (this morning, in a moment of despondency before sunrise), a prophetic density. Each word offers up a warning, I say to myself. I note the future of the change of heart. 'Instinct dictates duty' which is to say the future, which is to say the end and the revelation. But there might always be someone intelligent in me, as in J. D., who provides pretexts for eluding what is after all only a *duty* from the point of view of real life. At least, I say to myself, as a starting point for deciphering the secret book, the book afterwards named *Le Prénom de Dieu*, I've got some *hint* of the truth: *Le Lac*, this title, the letters spelled out in a firm hand to redeem the unfortunate foundling.

§

We can't stop here. I'll have to come back to it then, I say to myself. I convince myself that 'wisdom', something concrete, or plausible, an answer perhaps, will be brought to me by the Book, in a confrontation between the real object and the party of ghosts. On 4 August I decide to summon the dreaded Book. I dodge the few obstacles which, standing in my way at first, could be the pretext for evading the test. I am conscious of the fact that the circumstances, the date, are unfavourable for procuring an untraceable-book – libraries, bookshops, nothing lends itself to it. I don't doubt for a minute that Ange, and only she, must have a copy. She is in Paris at the time, as an attaché in a Ministry in that area of Saint-Germain that summer empties of its readings. I have in me the confidence that sustains William Legrand against all scepticism and, whereas not a soul on earth shares his fixation, neither the characters in his narrative nor the characters who read *The Gold-Bug*, for and because no one can believe it, the treasure *is found*, it was not a dream, as so often happens in all those novels despised by Baudelaire, where the author brutally awakens you 'after having excited your mind with tantalizing hopes'. This time the passage of time wavers along with the steadfastness of the Law. A sensation of Reality spreads across my study where the light and the concern for cleanliness come in. She sends it to me by the parcel service *Chronopost*. She doesn't need to tell me all the regulations she will have infringed to *dispatch* the Book to me, in broad daylight, at a forbidden hour, in a well-orchestrated fraud. I of all people should know that *Le Prénom de Dieu* is not for *dispatching*. Reticent Divinities are to be bought off. Now the book has gone. It is discharged from the Point of Departure.

౿

When I have only a day at the earliest, thirty-six hours at the latest to wait, a strange spirit of urgency takes hold of me, 'such that the mystery lives on' I say to myself 'such that I know not What awaits me': suddenly I find *the Courage* – or else I have exhausted the terrors – to want to answer the question: *Do you believe in the reality of this Gregor? Of this*

161

Gregor. And, breaking with the absolute impossibility of ever approaching 'reality' as current, programmed, in reality, by teletechnological operations, I go and consult the Pythias of the Web, I act with cold curiosity. Scientifically in truth this *Step* is a farewell that splices like a revolution. I expect something absolutely unimaginable. What drives me on is the desire to kill off the ghost. A pure, abstract desire, without strength, military, and which I obey with the submission without-self-state of the soldier *executing* the order for a *final* bout of hand-to-hand combat. (I realize, as soon as I perform the manoeuvre, that *never*, in my whole life, have I consulted the teletechnological Pythias. I think I can see a causal link between these two forms of abstention which until now did not seem to me to belong to the same geometric planes.) Did I think, whilst I was crawling amongst the undergrowth? I don't believe so. I don't know anymore whether we were trying to make sure to leave no trace. Or that there will have been traces. To sum up: there are brief instructions to be found by way of the name G. G. Someone by this sort of 'name' must have 'existed'. (I am not forgetting that this 'name' was a pseudonym.) That surprises me. This surprise makes me realize that I probably had someone in me, my mother perhaps, who had ended up no longer believing that this G. G. had some reality. But this outward reality is different from the false reality of the old G. G. in several respects. One of them surprises me – the character's date of birth. In the novel, the counterfeiter was born on the day war was declared in 1939 – a feature he had exploited in his other analyses. In the entry for him that comes up on the screen, neutral, brief, grey, wraithlike in its thinness, but which fits the earlier fiction for some elements (birthplace, language), sort of shrunken, the date of birth is the same as mine – an unspeakable detail – *to the day*. I look straight at the windowful of shadows. The man is declared a 'poet'. The most striking detail concerns the bibliography, for it includes *a single volume*. This volume is not called *Le Prénom de Dieu*. There is the following curiosity: that there is on the Web only the one person bearing this false name, in the relevant geographical area (North America). I don't know at what point I become aware of the article's heading, but the item falls into the category of '*Paid-notice: deaths*'. These are the obituary notices that appear in the big American newspapers, who decline all legal responsibility for them. It's a kind of fiction. It's well known that there are obituary notice organizations where you can get hold of made-up biographies to order, sometimes crude, but sometimes extraordinarily polished, elegant, and which are the work of young literature students recruited mainly in the Ivy League Universities and who constitute a secret society of highly adept writers, schooled in the study of classic texts, and highly knowledgeable. Imitators tinged with Edgar Poe or Emily Dickinson, or Melville, thus become inventors and beauticians of very interesting lives. These artists for the dead have a strange consolatory function – that there is nothing to stop them adding a little something in, since that's what they're paid for. You can even buy yourself a dead person. You can also join the society of young necromantic writers, declare yourself dead, follow your death with commentaries and lamentations. Fiction opens up all possibilities. Some can 'leave a considerable oeuvre' that will be available to posterity for fifty years. There is no limit to the realization of your desires.

I note that the shadow cast by G. G., if there was someone in reality behind these letters, is barely visible in the present – it slips faintly glistening in amongst the vast throng of shades loitering on the platform of the American Lethe. Like a pinch of dust. The summary gives off a dry aura that seems entirely threadbare, that could go unnoticed, which

163

was merely the presence, within the poverty of the remains, of one or two traces of the *extraordinary-manqué*. Here's one of them: G. G. was the illegitimate son of Narcisse Chaspoux, a dancer from the Paris Opera, and an unknown American doctor. It was from Narcisse that he'd got his musical genius. Says the little not-free announcement. Having been a child prodigy on the piano at the age of five, his move from Paris to New York had interrupted this prodigious destiny. After the fire at the Paris Opera all trace of these golden days has sadly disappeared. Says the paid announcement. I quickly examine these clues, so as to get at the secret source. It is noted first of all that a Narcisse Chaspoux 'existed'. And yet this person had an illegitimate son in the unfortunate Charles Meryon. Could it be that there was another Narcisse Chaspoux who was also a dancer at the Paris Opera? Certainly nothing is impossible but the improbability of it renders the homonymic hypothesis too fragile and too absurd to waste any time on it. The conclusion is clear and narrows the field of the investigation: the inventors must have known about the whole story of Meryon's turmoil. As for the aborted child prodigy, that's a recurrent motif in cases of family sagas – millions of still-born Mozarts haunt the limbo of millions of troubled minds. It only remains to find out who was the author of this character. Meryon, touched by the wand of hallucination, will have sadly ended his days like so many other denizens of indeterminate shores, in the company of Colonel Chabert. Nothing excludes our imagining that there was in 'Charenton' a 'society of writers' who were highly skilled in *creating* self-portraits. I shut down the computer and 'reality' once again offered up the appearance of true reality. Fiction takes its course

I look up at the sky. It is so clear on this morning, and I look up at this infinite, apparently blue fiction that I call 'sky'. 'Can you see the sky?' I said to J. D. on the telephone. I was imagining, as I said these words, that he was seeing the same sky. Here is where I resolve to put the trace of an oft-reworked memory: when J. D., just after the publication of the Book that I have been waiting for – it was just before me, so in 1965 (I am writing this in this today that becomes under my pen even a fiction) – advises me to change my name, to take a pseudonym, I immediately prepare to follow his advice. The choice quickly settles on the name of Jonas. I will have to come back to it, I say to myself. Pseudonym for pseudonym, my name is Jonas, for how long I can no longer remember.

Whilst I *wait* for the Book to get here, I want to see *Le Lac* one last time before the verdict. Only these signs. Instead of which, I forget why now, only now, perhaps because the circumstances lend my gaze an extra intensity of sublimity, upon opening the volume of typed stories, I can just make out, almost invisible beneath the title *La Baleine de Jonas*,[11] apparently in my hand and in pen, the title *itself*, in J. D.'s handwriting, in *pencil*. The stroke of the pen in black ink has merely almost entirely covered over the stroke of grey pencil. What caught my attention this time is the fleeting sense that the capital L that was the first letter of the title *La Baleine de Jonas* has something *different* about it. The fin of the hidden L still breaks the surface up by the flank of the black L and it's not mine. The first letters of the tablets of the Law are visible from a long way off. It moves you, because you 'know' that it's them, but you can't hear what they are saying. Why – when – how – had we – watched over – cloaked – the words

---

[11] *The Whale of Jonas.*

165

– summoned – by whom – by – what Law – or will – will I
ever know?

But my mother is 'reading' with enduring disquiet Jack
London's *History of Future Centuries*. Because she keeps won-
dering 'if it's made-up or if it's a true story', she can't move
on with her reading. She's keen to know what she's doing,
because that also conditions what she is. She wonders whether
she should *carry on* with the History of Future Centuries. In
this direction. Every time I go near her she speaks to me as if
to the teller at the truth counter: 'Tell me, this man, was he
an eye-witness to these events?' Before I reply I ask her what
difference that would make for her. 'Maybe it is a true story,'
says my mother. 'I hope so.' She says. 'It would make all the
difference in the world.' What battles we wage! At 99 years
of age we want to know 'whether all that is historical fact or
whether it's just-a-story.' 'I don't know whether it's a true
story.' 'This Jack, was he a witness to everything that happened *out there*? *In the future centuries*? Maybe he was already
right in the future?' She turns to me. 'He wrote and it was
prophetic,' she worries. 'People write,' I say, 'and it's prophetic. But there is no prophet,' I say, '*in reality*, all prophets
are false prophets, which makes no difference at all, because
all realities are fictions.' I say. 'Have you read *Martin Eden*?'
asks my mother. 'I think Martin Eden was the author of this
Jack London,' I say. 'That Martin Eden was really something,' says my mother. 'Truly. How am I supposed to read
people who want to *change* the world?'

8

The Book doesn't arrive. That's so like it, I say to myself.
It's quite natural. I see the postman pass by twice on the

horizon without stopping. He is part of the old stock of the species of messages that govern the laws of the Mishap. I say to myself. You *wait* for them; you expect them to arrive; they don't arrive; you don't expect them not to arrive. How much trust we have. It is created only for treachery. One day when I spend all my time protecting Henry from the numerous attempted murders that lie in wait for him in airports, in the vestibules of big hotels where malevolent emissaries lurk, as he is trying to make himself heard to an inattentive customs officer in amongst a group of ruthless patrons, so as to cover his back that is so vulnerable against any knocks, I clasp myself to him, to make him feel better, and it's precisely this well-meaning pressure that forces a cry of pain from him. I *believed* that the Book would arrive. The last copy. It's a jinx, at least where I'm concerned. I say to myself.

When Ange starts to fret that her book might have been lost, after having been preserved except for thirty years on her bookshelves, I reply: it's not *your* book, it's mine. It's not your distress. It's *my distress* that ought to be pitied. She refuses to hear it.

On reflection I can see that this scene is a *grotesque* reproduction of the pastiche of the pastiche of *Pelléas et Mélisande* where Marcel Proust laments the loss of *his* hat, it was forever lost to the great consternation of that Markel Proust. 'It was a poor little hat, one could not have said where it came from . . . it seemed to come from the end of the world . . . !' How ridiculous suffering is! I say to myself. What suffering! As a pastiche, it only exasperates my distress. Now, I say to Ange, we'll have to give up the search, 'because we wouldn't find it'. It was a little yellowed book, it seemed to come from the end of the world, one could not have said where it came from. You made a mistake in sending that volume! Someone not from here, but perhaps from the house of Chronos, will have taken it and God knows where it is now. I feel as though I have taken leave of myself.

I was sure that the Book wouldn't get here, I say. I expected as much. And yet I couldn't *believe* that it wouldn't arrive.

One of the effects that the faraway Book as such produces is discord (revulsion, revolt). It's an extremely violent, but not externalized affect. You hit out at yourself and at others indiscriminately, you are bitten and you bite, all this in your imagination and in dreams – everything bites. Fear takes shape in the corners of the mouth. For a whole week I dreamt that I was no longer living. One night when I go into the study barefoot with a dream in my hand in the dark so as to set it down on paper without waking it, suddenly something moving grabs hold of my foot and closes its jaws around my toes. I scream. The cry of an animal caught in a snare. I let go of the dream. I fumble for the light switch. It's a box. It's lying on its back, and I must have stood on it, knocked into it, it grips my foot with all its legs and all its mandibles – how many I couldn't say. It's bronzed black and extraordinarily large. We stand stock-still. I guess that it is as frightened as I am. It is fastened to my foot for eternity, if necessary. I don't know how, but with a powerful wrench, I break free of its grip; without a moment's hesitation I arm myself with the broom that stands guard in the cupboard. I note that the beast, for its part, has not moved. As if it were asleep on its back with its dozens of feet clasped around the shadow of my foot. Gently, I sweep it slowly towards the end of the world and I don't see it disappear off into the night. One could not have said where it came from. Its bite didn't break the skin. It's the number of scratches from its dozens of feet that marked me. Markel:

'One never finds anything again . . . here . . . .' These words from Markel haunt me: a suspended sentence . . .

Here I remember that William Legrand's friend also never stopped saying and thinking that it was time to abandon the search. This Gold-Bug. Someone with good sense: the realization that the so-called gold-bug was not gold. It was a fake gold-bug. A dead bug in truth. Edgar le Garde, the guard, makes me think of adding to the treasure: must take into account the complications that the presence of the bug introduces as a part-time hunter 'into the very principle of calculability'. Had it not been for the fake gold-bug, which is to say the truly dead bug, would William Legrand – would he not – have been able to find the real treasure? The bug as real and as illusion – that is, the *Bug*.

Bug: put here the complications owing to the Bug

(1) as a substitute in translation, so as a translated remainder, of the original subject in English whose name is *Bug*. Account will have to be taken here of the disruptions introduced into the fantastical global network by the '*current*' use of the word bug, in the world of IT. The value bug is subjected to immense and almost paradoxical variations depending on whether it be considered as in Ka in Egypt, or as in the bungling dung beetle in the West. Always drawn to the letter, we have opted for the scarabesque, which is to say the Baudelairesque.

(2) in truth the useless but necessary bug, signed 'Death's Head', and which has nothing to do with the treasure, unless there has been some *illusion*, is also wonderfully part of the treasure since it has the appearance of being so, when it

partakes of and belongs to the narrative as a whole on the one hand, the treasure on the other, intrinsically, extrinsically, insectly, as a vital deceptor.

This bug belongs to no one. It is pure death. No one has lost it. It belongs to God, it belongs only to God, and it is God's turd.

It gives all that it hasn't got and what it is not, says Henry.

This bug is taboo. It is Contaminated. It traps all the craziest thoughts. It is a fearstone.

Still the inexplicable left: the bug's *weight*. The insect was remarkably heavy, which I could not understand in reality. The whole thing will have revolved around this weight. Had it been a matter of my own life, I would not have found the *key* to the riddle, if there has to be just the one. In my view, what makes it so heavy can only be 'death'. Though we still have to agree on what we call *death*. Is the box that bites me alive or dead? The little Book that doesn't arrive cannot be said not to be driven by an intention or at least by some instinct or other.

So I *thought*: may as well *forget* the Box. Try to forget – what an idea! I will never again shake off its claws. Besides, the thought of managing to forget the Box was hideous. Not that I would wish at all costs to make it public. But I now had a dream lain in a meagre cradle hanging over the balcony – where the geraniums are – a tiny little child that faintly whimpers at night time as if it dared not complain but could not stifle its infinite sorrow. But if I took it up once more, if I accepted it if I opened up the chest, if I study it, if I analyse it, I examine it, I file it, I compare it, I carefully dissect it, where will that all lead? Besides, the Bug is hopeless. That won't have stopped the seekers from being led to the treasure. On the contrary. Making false into true would have been futile without the dead weight.

And I looked up at the Sky in vain. Illegible. On the Thursday I want to try. I can't get up – a Dizzy spell overwhelms me. This time It's not on its back. I am felled, jostled, shoved against the farthest wall from the Box. I wonder if I should consider this assault against me as a sign of revenge. A protest by the Silent one against the decision to abandon it – the Box, that is – or *Le Prénom de Dieu*'s secret. When I think that for J. D. all that was literature I am filled with melancholy. I would have very much liked to have been able to read instead of being possessed without possessing. In the daytime the Box is now emitting an insect-like buzzing sound.

In the end, after quite a storm, one fine morning and without warning, the ending presents itself so clearly that all misgivings melt away like ghosts at dawn: I decide to destroy the Box. I was right not to talk to my archikeeper about it, I say to myself. I imagine the scene. Had I done so – my first impulse having been to donate it all to the Bibliothèque Nationale de France – I would now have to exonerate myself, which couldn't be done. You can't make a gift of poisoned leftovers, I say to myself. I can already see a chapter on behalf of the defence brewing. As it happens, I had already held back at the last extremity of this covenant on the future. The Wind outside pastiches: I'm sweeping! I'm sweeping! 'Yes, yes I know, I heard!'

All that remains is to select the method of elimination. Naturally, fire would be what first springs to mind, and it was: 'burn the letters'. Having never burned letter nor document in my life, I am tempted – that would be new. But I don't listen to this thought. That wouldn't reckon on the ghosts born of ashes. They are so skittish that no one can ever escape them. Anyway, I say to myself, I can't condemn a soul to the stake. I wouldn't survive that.

Burial, drowning – these solutions present themselves and are dismissed. Because you've no idea how heavy the body of a Box that's been outthought is. Besides which, I'm tiring of the struggle. But one Sunday morning, I hear at last the final rumble. 'What's that noise?' says my mother. 'The binmen!' I shout. It's one of the peculiarities of this little town to send the procession of rubbish trucks out on Sunday mornings. 'The rubbish truck's coming!' I shouted. (I don't say bins because she wouldn't have time to hear such a short word.) 'It's a dreadful thing,' says my mother.

But for me, it's a blessing. I quickly set the Box down in front of the door. How dull and clean it is. There is none like it. That'll give it some chance. This way I won't have seen to its disappearance – at least that's how I think of it. Have a good trip, I say. I said have a good trip in a very low voice, very near silence. I didn't want a passerby to overhear me, but I wanted to be clearly heard by the gods.

'And what's that noise?' says my mother. 'It's the trucks coming to take away the remains,' I say. This way, I say to myself, my train of thought following along behind the heavy rumble of the chariot, Destiny will decide for this Remainder, what will be will be, and God knows where his first name is now. I go into the empty house. I expect to weep.

While I am waiting I write the following tears: ♭ ♬ ♩ ♪ ♫ ♪ ♪ ♪ ♭ ♭ ♪ ♪